The Ku Klux Klan

Guides to
Subcultures and
Countercultures

The
Ku Klux Klan

A Guide to an American Subculture

Martin Gitlin

GREENWOOD PRESS
An Imprint of ABC-CLIO, LLC

A B C ● C L I O

Santa Barbara, California • Denver, Colorado • Oxford, England

Library of Congress Cataloging-in-Publication Data

Gitlin, Martin.
   The Ku Klux Klan / Martin Gitlin.
      p. cm. — Guides to subcultures and countercultures
   Includes bibliographical references and index.
   ISBN 978-0-313-36576-8 (hard copy : alk. paper) — ISBN 978-0-313-36577-5 (ebook)
1. Ku Klux Klan (19th cent.) 2. Ku Klux Klan (1915-)
3. Racism—United States—History. 4. Hate groups—United States—History.
5. United States—Race relations. I. Title.
   HS2330.K63G54   2009
   332.4′20973–dc22   2009022122

13   12   11   10   09   1   2   3   4   5

This book is also available on the World Wide Web as an eBook.
Visit www.abc-clio.com for details.

ABC-CLIO, LLC
130 Cremona Drive, P.O. Box 1911
Santa Barbara, California 93116-1911

This book is printed on acid-free paper ∞

Manufactured in the United States of America

Contents

Series Foreword

From Beatniks to Flappers, Zoot Suiters to Punks, this series brings to life some of the most compelling countercultures in American history. Designed to offer a quick, in-depth examination and current perspective on each group, the series aims to stimulate the reader's understanding of the richness of the American experience. Each book explores a countercultural group critical to American life and introduces the reader to its historical setting and precedents, the ways in which it was subversive or countercultural, and its significance and legacy in American history. *Webster's Ninth New Collegiate Dictionary* defines counterculture as "a culture with values and mores that run counter to those of established society." Although some of the groups covered can be described as primarily subcultural, they were targeted for inclusion because they have not existed in a vacuum. They have advocated for rules that methodically opposed mainstream culture, or they have lived by their ideals to the degree that it became impossible not to impact the society around them. They have left their marks, both positive and negative, on the fabric of American culture. Volumes cover such groups as Hippies and Beatniks, who impacted popular culture, literature, and art; the Eco-Socialists and Radical

Feminists, who worked toward social and political change; and even groups such as the Ku Klux Klan, who left mostly scars.

A lively alternative to narrow historiography and scholarly monographs, each volume in the *Subcultures and Countercultures* series can be described as a "library in a book," containing both essays and browsable reference materials, including primary documents, to enhance the research process and bring the content alive in a variety of ways. Written for students and general readers, each volume includes engaging illustrations, a timeline of critical events in the subculture, topical essays that illuminate aspects of the subculture, a glossary of subculture terms and slang, biographical sketches of the key players involved, and primary source excerpts—including speeches, writings, articles, first-person accounts, memoirs, diaries, government reports, and court decisions—that offer contemporary perspectives on each group. In addition, each volume includes an extensive bibliography of current recommended print and nonprint sources appropriate for further research.

Preface

The Spanish philosopher Santayana once exclaimed that those who forget the past are condemned to repeat it. It became his most famous utterance, perhaps the most significant in history in regard to the importance of history.

There are many reasons to write about the Ku Klux Klan (KKK; Klan)—both past and present. Their outrageous image and regalia, the perceived dangerousness of their worldview, and their violent tendencies all make the KKK a curiosity and an interesting topic. But more important is that it allows us to follow the advice of Santayana to learn about the past to create a more peaceful future.

In a nation that embraces freedom of opinion and action only until it infringes on the freedom of others, extremist organizations are destined to exist and are even given the opportunity to flourish, as did the Klan for a decade early in the twentieth century. However, that same freedom of expression exposes Americans to hundreds of groups and philosophies, which in turn reduces the likelihood that a radical and violent right-wing organization such as the Klan will gain significant power.

Therefore, this book is not to be considered a warning against the possibility that the Ku Klux Klan or its reactionary descendents in the military racist and anti-Semitic movements are poised to take over the United States. Rather, it is a detailed history of the KKK and an examination of the events that steered its philosophies and actions. In addition, the huge majority of Americans would consider it beneficial to gain a greater understanding of the Klan so that they could help in some way to prevent instances of the violence and murder for which it gained fame and notoriety.

This book has been arranged in chronological order, detailing the various eras of the Klan from its founding just months after the ending of the Civil War to the present. It intends to offer insight into the Klan's history, behavior, and methodology, including coverage of the role of women in the Klan, media coverage of the Klan, and Klan philosophy. It also includes biographies of particularly colorful and influential Klan leaders over the years, selected primary document excerpts of writings by and about Klan members, and a glossary of the organization's unique vocabulary.

Americans have traditionally been fascinated with extremist organizations, but only from afar. The lone era in which the Klan successfully passed itself off as a group truly espousing righteousness was between 1915 and 1925, during which time it toned down its violence and attracted millions of members. Aside from that period, it has gained a reputation for luring only the angry and downtrodden of American society.

Though Klansmen and their leaders have generally wrapped their racist and anti-Semitic views around what they perceive as logic, most experts believe those hatreds have been greatly based on personal fear. It is widely accepted that their embracing of white supremacy is based on ignorance. But it is less understood that because Klansmen have been generally in the lowest financial strata in American society, they have felt threatened by blacks who have struggled for and gained equal rights and opportunities.

Similarly, their anti-Semitic views are not merely based on half-baked interpretations of Biblical messages that Jews are the Devil's apostles. They are far more driven by simple prejudice and the acceptance of the extremist view that Jews control the economy and are keeping them from securing their rightful piece of the American dream.

Dozens of sources were used to research this book. But despite that, a common thread ran through all of the historical examinations of the Ku Klux Klan—its basic philosophies and motivations haven't changed in 150 years in a nation that has changed dramatically during that same period. That is why at the time this book was written, the popularity of the Klan had arguably plummeted to the lowest level in history. But those who believe the Klan could never rise again should take heed of its past revivals and remember the wise words of George Santayana.

Klan Timeline

December 24, 1865 Six former Confederate officers meet at the law offices of Calvin Jones to discuss forming a club. The Ku Klux Klan is born.

1866 Tennessee Klansmen begin taking violent measures in an attempt to control black independence.

April 1867 Former Confederate General Nathan Bedford Forrest is named Grand Wizard.

Fall 1867 Tennessee Klansmen commit twenty-five murders and thirty-five assaults with intent to kill against blacks and whites supporting Reconstruction.

October 1868 In an interview with the *Cincinnati Commercial*, Forrest claims that the Klan now boasts 550,000 members throughout the South. The article motivates the United States government to take action against the Klan.

January 1869   Forrest issues the order for disbandment of the Klan, which serves only to disassociate himself from the organization as Klan violence continues.

March 30, 1870   The Fifteenth Amendment gives blacks the right to vote, prompting Klansmen to pressure blacks into voting against Republicans.

April 20, 1871   The House passes a bill stating that American citizens could sue others for depriving them of rights guaranteed by the Constitution.

1871   Mississippi Klansmen kill several blacks during a trial of blacks accused of civil unrest in the demands to vote.

1873   The government enforcement policy eliminates Klan activity, but the enactment of Jim Crow laws in the South makes their efforts unnecessary.

1896   The Supreme Court decision in the *Plessy v. Ferguson* case legitimizes segregation in the South.

January 8, 1915   The premiere in Los Angeles of the D.W. Griffith blockbuster film *Birth of a Nation* portrays Klansmen as heroes and blacks as animalistic. The film is seen by 25 million Americans, including an impressed President Woodrow Wilson, and inspires the second Klan era.

April 27, 1915   Fourteen-year-old Mary Phagan, an employee at a Georgia pencil factory, is found raped and murdered. Jewish factory owner Leo Frank is convicted of the crime despite unsubstantial evidence. His death sentenced is reduced to life imprisonment, motivating a mob to abduct and hang him. The incident is believed by many to be a precursor to the reestablishment of the Klan.

Thanksgiving 1915 William Simmons revives the Ku Klux Klan in a cross-burning ceremony on Stone Mountain near Atlanta.

June 7, 1920 Southern Publicity Association business partners Thomas Clarke and Elizabeth Tyler are hired to further the Klan cause and launch a membership drive. The result is by far the most significant growth in the history of the organization.

September 6, 1921 The *New York World* launches a two-week exposé into Klan activities and publishes an account of 152 Klan crimes. The syndicated accounts are detailed in eighteen other national newspapers and calls for a government investigation into the organization.

October 10, 1921 Simmons, who has sent telegrams to every member of the House urging them to vote not to censure the Klan, begins testifying to the Committee of Rules. He claims that the Klan is neither racist nor violent. Congress drops the investigation, thereby giving the Klan its stamp of approval. The resulting publicity adds hundreds of thousands of new members throughout the country.

November 1922 Simmons is stripped of his position as Imperial Wizard by Hiram Wesley Evans during the annual Klonvocation in Atlanta.

1924 Klan membership peaks at over 4 million.

March 25, 1925 Charismatic and popular Indiana Klan leader David Curtis Stephenson rapes and attacks female acquaintance Marge Oberholtzer, who commits suicide as she suffered from kidney failure as a result of the attack. The subsequent publicity lands Stephenson in jail and sends Klan membership reeling.

August 8, 1925	Klansmen are disappointed as only 30,000 show up to a march in Washington, D.C. Heavy rains and a lack of attendance signal the end of strong Klan influence in America.
1930	National Klan membership has fallen 90 percent to 45,000.
March 1931	Fourteen Klansmen abduct and whip two Communist organizers in Dallas for speaking out in favor of black equality and against the practice of lynching. During the Depression, the Klan launches a campaign of terror against suspected Communists.
April 1934	Citrus Workers organizer Frank Norman is abducted by Klansmen in Lakeland, Florida, and is never seen again.
1936	Evans liquidates most of the Klan real estate, including the Imperial Palace, due to financial hardship. A lack of membership and the Great Depression are blamed.
June 10, 1939	James Colescott becomes the first Klan Imperial Wizard who rose through the ranks.
1939	American Nazi Party leader Fritz Kuhn unsuccessfully attempts to combine his organization with the Klan.
1939–1940	Atlanta-area Klansmen launch a wave of violent floggings of perceived political enemies.
Spring 1944	The Internal Revenue Service reveals that the Klan had yet to pay $685,000 in back taxes. Colescott is forced to disband the organization, though some Klaverns remain active.
Spring 1946	Advertisements in Atlanta newspapers trumpet another Klan revival. Three hundred

new members are sworn in during a ceremony on Stone Mountain.

December 5, 1946 President Harry Truman creates an executive commission on human rights in an attempt to prevent a postwar Klan revival, but the Klan begins to flourish again in the Deep South.

November 1948 Strong Klan supporter Herman Talmadge is elected governor of Georgia.

December 25, 1951 A series of Klan bombings in Miami that destroys black homes, Jewish synagogues, and Catholic churches culminates in the bombing of the home of Harry T. Moore, a superintendent of public instruction and head of Florida's National Association for the Advancement of Colored People (NAACP).

May 17, 1954 The Supreme Court decision in the *Brown v. Board of Education* case bans school segregation, setting off the civil rights movement and ushering in an era of Klan expansion and greater violence.

September 1956 New Imperial Wizard leader Eldon Edwards hosts a cross-burning ceremony on Stone Mountain with a huge crowd of 1,500 attending.

January 1957 Klansmen bomb four black churches and several black residences in Montgomery, Alabama, after Reverend Martin Luther King, Jr. organized the successful bus boycott.

September 1957 Alabama Klansmen led by Asa Carter abduct and castrate black handyman Edward Aaron in one of the most racially charged hate crimes in American history. The four perpetrators were found guilty and sentenced to twenty years in prison, but were paroled by Alabama governor George Wallace in 1963.

February 1960   The first "sit-in" is staged at a Woolworth's lunch counter in Greensboro, North Carolina, by seventeen-year-old student McNeil Joseph. The tactic to call attention to segregation in public places is picked up by the Congress of Racial Equality (CORE) and Student Nonviolent Coordinating Committee (SNCC) and soon spreads to sixty-eight cities across the South. Klansmen react with violence.

January 1961   Klan membership soars to over 20,000.

February 1961   "Wild Bill" Davidson and Calvin Craig found the Invisible Empire, United Klans, Knights of the Ku Klux Klan of America, Inc. Robert Shelton soon takes over as its Imperial Wizard.

October 1, 1962   Klansmen converge on the University of Mississippi to prevent admission of black student James Meredith. White students and out-of-state demonstrators join them as two people are killed in the ensuing violence.

September 15, 1963 Klansman Robert Chambliss and accomplices bomb the Sixteenth Street Baptist Church in Birmingham, Alabama, killing four black girls. Chambliss isn't convicted and sent to jail until 1977.

June 21, 1964   Civil rights workers Michael "Mickey" Schwerner, Andrew Goodman, and James Chaney are murdered by Klansman in Mississippi with the complicity and participation of Neshoba County lawmen. Their bodies are found two months later in an earthen dam. The FBI gathers overwhelming evidence against the Klansmen, but

Mississippi authorities are unwilling to act. Federal authorities send the Klansmen to jail two years later on charges that they deprived the civil rights workers of their civil rights.

July 11, 1964

Klansmen murder black army officer Lemuel Penn on a highway near Athens, Georgia. He was mistaken for being a civil rights worker.

March 9, 1965

James Reeb, a Unitarian minister from Boston, is beaten to death in Selma, Alabama, by Klansmen wielding clubs and lead pipes. Reeb was in town to participate in protests against police violence in Selma.

March 25, 1965

Selma, Alabama, Klansmen shoot and kill Detroit housewife Viola Liuzzo while she is driving a car and injure passenger LeRoy Moton. Liuzzo was inspired to travel to Selma to participate in a march that day after hearing about the murder of Reeb on television. The Liuzzo murder prompts President Johnson to order Congress to launch a complete investigation of the Klan.

Fall 1968

Alabama governor and presidential candidate George Wallace praises the Klan and welcomes its support during his campaign, claiming during the height of the Vietnam War that at least Klansmen would fight for their country.

1969

Klan membership shrinks to 7,000 from a peak of 40,000 in 1965.

1974

Klan membership falls to an all-time low of 1,500 before David Duke takes over leadership of the Louisiana Knights of the Ku Klux Klan and espouses a cleaner look and political activism. He is quickly named Imperial Wizard of the White Knights of the Ku Klux Klan. Meanwhile, issues such as busing and affirmative action begin to bring in a new generation of Klansmen.

1975   Duke names four new Grand Dragons: Tom Metzger (California), Don Black (Alabama), Louis Beam (Texas), and Bill Wilkinson (Louisiana). The latter two prove to have far more violent philosophies than Duke.

1978–1979   Klan membership jumps 25 percent.

February 1979   An estimated 150 robed Klansmen drive through Decatur, Alabama, waving shotguns and pistols during a march held by blacks protesting the rape conviction of a severely retarded black man. The Klansmen battle police and go on a shooting spree. Three marchers and two Klansmen are shot. Nine Klansmen are eventually indicted, including several Alabama Klan leaders.

November 3, 1979   Klansmen murder five members of the Communist Workers Party (CWP) during a CWP demonstration in Greensboro, North Carolina. An all-white jury acquits the Klansmen, arguing that they reacted in self-defense.

July 1980   Three Klansmen drive through Chattanooga, Tennessee, and indiscriminately shoot five black women, including one planting flowers in her front lawn. Following the acquittal of two of the Klansmen and the conviction of the third on minor charges, young blacks in Chattanooga riot for three consecutive nights.

March 21, 1981   Mobile, Alabama, Klansmen abduct, strangle, and hang nineteen-year-old black man Michael Donald.

1981   Metzger leaves the Klan to form the White American Political Association, which later morphs into White Aryan Resistance (WAR). Duke leaves the Klan to form the National Association for the Advancement of White People (NAAWP).

July 28, 1983   Klansmen break into the Southern Poverty Law Center and firebomb the offices of Klanwatch. Funds pour in from throughout the nation to build a new fireproof and bombproof building.

1987   A wrongful death suit filed by the mother of Michael Donald results in a $7 million verdict against the United Klans of America. Klansman Henry Hays is convicted of murder and is executed on June 6, 1997. He is the first Klansman to be sentenced to death for the murder of a black.

June 20–21, 1995   Two black churches in South Carolina are destroyed by fire. Klansmen Gary Cox and Timothy Welch plead guilty to setting the fires in August 1996. In 1998, the Christian Knights of the KKK and South Carolina Grand Dragon Horace King are ordered to pay $37.8 million in damages for the burning of the Macedonia Baptist Church.

October 27, 1996   Klansman Joshua Kennedy fires eleven times into a crowd of black teenagers in South Carolina, wounding three. In 1998, he is sentenced to twenty-six years in prison.

August 21, 1998   Former Klan leader Sam Bowers is convicted of ordering a firebombing of the home of civil rights leader Vernon Dahmer

	in 1966. He is sent to prison, where he dies in November 2006.
October 23, 1999	An estimated 6,000 counter-demonstrators protest against a KKK rally in New York City.
May 17, 2000	Former Klansmen Thomas Blanton, Jr. and Bobby Frank Cherry are indicted and later convicted for their roles in the 1963 bombing of a Birmingham, Alabama, church that killed four young black girls. Both are sentenced to life in prison.
June 23, 2005	One-time Klansman Edgar Ray Killen is sentenced to sixty years in jail for his part in the 1964 slaying of three civil rights workers in Mississippi.
November 9, 2008	Klansman Raymond Foster shoots and kills an Oklahoma woman whom he lured over the Internet to take part in a KKK initiation. Her body is found on a country road. Foster is convicted of second-degree murder and sent to prison.

Origin of the
KKK

The ink had barely dried on the document signed by General Robert
E. Lee at the Appomattox Court House confirming the surrender of
the Confederate Army and signaling the end of the Civil War. The
stench of death had been cleared only recently from the towns, fields,
and backwoods of America. Bodies riddled with bullet holes were still
being discovered. Mothers and wives, sons and daughters, and brothers and sisters of fallen soldiers still shed tears of grief.

Among the hundreds of Southern cities and villages lamenting
the demise of the Confederacy and the slave-holding business that
fueled the area economy was Pulaski, Tennessee. Though many people from Confederate states outside the deep South felt apathetic
about or even supported the end of slavery, few inhabited Pulaski, a
major slave-holding town neighboring the Alabama border whose
citizens were proud of its stately manors and beautiful plantations, as
well as what they deemed to be the purity of their Scottish ancestry.

It was December 24, 1865. Though a cyclone had recently ripped
through Pulaski, destroying several homes and plantations, its children
eagerly awaited the opportunity to open Christmas presents the following morning. Their parents looked forward to a holiday that could

finally bring joy to their lives, which had been so badly shaken by the war and its consequences. But in the Pulaski law office of Calvin Jones, six men who would eventually reveal far more sinister plans were about to meet.

Jones was joined by James Crowe, Richard Reed, John Lester, Frank McCord, and John Kennedy. All were former army officers who had fought bravely and were fiercely loyal to their perception of the Confederate cause. Kennedy had been shot three times and taken prisoner. Crowe, too, had recovered from gunshot wounds. The other four had served with the Tennessee infantry. All were well educated for the times; in fact, four of them were studying to become lawyers, McCord was a writer who would soon be hired as the editor of the town newspaper, and Lester's political ambitions would land him in the Tennessee legislature.

In the aftermath of the war, they were all angry and bored. Pulaski was under the authority of Tennessee Provisional Governor William G. Brownlow, a Methodist minister with fanatical anti-Confederate and anti-slavery feelings. The six who met in Jones' law office on that Christmas Eve felt frustrated at the notion that their beloved South could never return to what they considered to be its glory days—dependent on the slave trade to thrive economically and founded on belief in the inherent inequality of the races. They believed that something had to be done, so Lester suggested that the group form a club. The others agreed and soon a committee of three was created to decide on a name for the tiny new organization while the others set out to draft a set of rules.

Though the dates of subsequent meetings remain sketchy, it is known that the six later met at the mansion of Colonel Thomas Martin, another former Confederate officer from Pulaski, who had asked Kennedy to housesit for him while he was out of town. When they reconvened, the best that the naming committee could come up with for the fledgling club was "the circle," which indicates that they hadn't given it much thought. Kennedy suggested that to give the name a bit more sparkle, they should change the word "circle" into the Greek translation: kuklos.

"Call it kuklux," Crowe chirped, "and no one will know what it means."

"And add klan," Kennedy followed, "as we are all of Scotch-Irish descent."[1]

The Ku Klux Klan (Klan or KKK) was born. Thus inspired, the brainstorming Pulaski Six (as they became known) searched Mrs. Martin's linen closet for proper attire. They pulled pillowcases over their heads and draped themselves in white sheets, then left the house on horseback and raised a din, riding around town to the curiosity and amusement of their fellow citizens. The group enjoyed and promoted its image as town spooks. The six cultivated that image by wearing long, loose-fitting white gowns adorned with various bright-red occult symbols such as half-moons and stars. They slid white cloth witches' hats over their faces, hiding everything but their eyes, which they believed gave them an even more mysterious presentation. The cone-shaped headwear raised the height of the individual Klan members nearly two feet, adding a frightening aura to their images.

Meanwhile, the rules committee was busily matching the strange and mysterious outfits with strange and mysterious titles for the offices it created. McCord would serve as the Grand Cyclops (president) with Kennedy as the Grand Magi (vice-president). Crowe was deemed the Grand Turk, McCord's assistant. The others, called Night Hawks, were to protect the group from outside interference. The rules committee created no stated purpose for the Ku Klux Klan. At first, it was intended to be merely an apolitical social organization whose members were obligated only to "have fun, make mischief, and play pranks on the public."[2]

That they did. The Pulaski Six would ride through the town at night in their skeleton robes, clanging chains and entertaining the citizenry. It's no wonder in the depressed post-war environment that the locals received them openly and joyously. It's also not surprising that the Ku Klux Klan membership grew rapidly and exponentially.

But soon the members were bored with business as usual. The mindless pranks on fellow townspeople they respected and with whom they felt much in common no longer brought excitement to the Klansmen. The initiations had become old hat. They decided to turn their attention to recently emancipated blacks and their families. The plan was to terrorize the former slaves, many of whom were superstitious and wholly uneducated, by wearing their white robes and caps and convincing them that they were the ghosts of dead Confederate soldiers and citizens who were returning to seek revenge on the freedmen. Lester claimed that on occasion Klansmen pulled their robes over their heads and placed false heads on top. They then removed the false heads and handed them to blacks, requesting that they hold on to them for a while. According to legend fueled by Klansmen, the blacks would then run screaming into the night.

Another Klan gag required a bit more imagination. Klansmen would attach to their chests an oilskin bag with a siphon tube running up to their masks. An article in the *Louisiana Planters Banner* explained the rest:

> A night traveler called at the Negro quarters . . . and asked for water. After he had drunk three blue buckets full of good cistern water, at which the Negro was astonished, he thanked the colored man and told him he was very thirsty, that he had traveled nearly a thousand miles in twenty-four hours, and that was the best drink of water he had had since he was killed at the battle of Shiloh. The Negro dropped the bucket, tumbled over two chairs and a table, escaped through a back window, and has not been heard from.[3]

Although negative stereotypes perpetrated about black gullibility motivated Klansmen to believe they were truly frightening them with such scare tactics, later evidence indicated otherwise. In testimony to legislative committees, blacks who had been the victims of such stunts claimed they knew all along that white men were behind them. In fact, some added that they recognized the voices of former slave masters and white neighbors behind the masks. Nevertheless, the practical jokes proved to be just the first phase of Klan intimidation against blacks. The Tennessee Klan began the next step in late 1866 by attempting to control black independence. Klan night-riding groups with such colorful names as the Yellow Jackets and Redcaps would suddenly appear to break up black prayer meetings or social functions, as well as raid homes and steal firearms.

Klan violence started soon after former Confederate General Nathan Bedford Forrest was named Grand Wizard in 1867. Forrest, who was crippled by gunfire during the Civil War, had been a millionaire plantation owner, but the abolition of slavery wrecked him financially and embittered him toward freed slaves. Forrest not only recruited new members throughout the South, but he reorganized the KKK geographically. The combination of empowerment within the organization and anger over the changes in the political landscape, including the right to vote for newly enfranchised blacks, motivated Klansmen to take the law into their own hands. They terrorized not only blacks, but also white teachers working with black students and representatives of Northern-based organizations such as the Union League, which was schooling freed slaves about the voting process.

Among the new Klan designations was the Ghoul, who represented the lowest rung of the organizational hierarchy and ranked below such authorities as the Grand Dragon, Giant, Cyclops and Night Hawk. But though they boasted no clout in the Klan, they were greatly responsible for doing the dirty work in the local communities. Secret society expert Shelley Klein wrote:

> They beat, shot, stabbed, and hanged their victims without a hint of conscience, forming vigilante groups to target non-white people who were accused of breaking the law [although their supposed "crimes" might be as innocuous as appearing not to show enough respect to their white neighbors], who belonged to political organizations, or who were audacious enough to purchase their own land or business. The KKK also aimed their focus on any whites who were thought to be aiding and abetting their black neighbors. This could include white teachers who taught in black schools, white businessmen working with black colleagues, or anyone found "guilty" of giving a black person preferential treatment over a white person.[4]

During a five-month period in the summer and early fall of 1867, it was reported by the Union League that the Tennessee Klan had committed twenty-five murders, thirty-five assaults with the intent to kill, eighty-three assault and batteries, four rapes, and four arsons. Klansmen began an ominous new tactic of leaving threatening notes for their planned victims. And while Republican supporters such as the Union League attempted to better the lives of blacks, many Democrats embraced the KKK and much of the media followed suit. The editor of Virginia's *Richmond Examiner* went so far as to write, "under its cap and bells (the Klan) hides a purpose as resolute, noble and heroic as that which Brutus concealed beneath the mask of well-dissembled idiocy. It is rapidly organizing wherever the insolent

Negro, the malignant white traitor to his race, and the infamous squatter are plotting to make the South utterly unfit for the residence of the decent white man."[5]

Word of KKK intimidation and violence spread north, whereupon the Freedmen's Bureau, a federal agency established after the Civil War to help blacks blend into society, sprang into action. Inspector Joseph W. Gelray was sent to Tennessee to investigate. He discovered that John Dunlap, a white teacher at a black school, had been whipped and informed that if he didn't leave town, he would be burned at the stake. Gelray learned of Mrs. Lewis Powell, a black woman who had been shot to death for working with the Union League. He heard about a group of blacks at a prayer meeting who were badly beaten by KKK thugs. And, greatly disturbing to Gelray, he saw no evidence of civil authorities or fellow citizens taking steps to prevent such violence or arrest the perpetrators. They were either too fearful or silently backed the hooded vigilantes. In some cases, the law and the KKK were one in the same. The result was that many blacks moved to major cities in the South, where the Klan had not yet been established.

The free hand his organization enjoyed prompted the overconfident Forrest to grant an interview with the *Cincinnati Commercial* in late 1868 that proved to be a tactical error. The KKK could literally get away with murder in Tennessee and the Deep South, greatly because of their sympathetic fellow citizens. But the newspaper article served to awaken the United States government to its revolutionary intent and widespread following. Forrest claimed the KKK to be a military organization that now numbered 40,000 in Tennessee alone and 550,000 throughout the South. He claimed that the Klan was growing not only in Tennessee, but in Alabama and Mississippi as well. In fact, he boasted that there were also chapters in rural areas of Kentucky, Virginia, West Virginia, South Carolina, and Georgia.

Soon President Andrew Johnson was called on to take action. But though he made federal troops available to local authorities, Klan activity continued virtually unabated into the 1870s. However, Forrest's admissions brought awareness to the brutality of its members. In addition, the mushrooming of the KKK throughout the South proved to weaken central jurisdiction. Ghouls representing individual dens in various states did whatever they pleased. Even Forrest was displeased with the lack of authority emanating from the Imperial Headquarters in Memphis. So in late January 1869, he issued an order that called for the disbandment of the Klan and ordered that all masks and costumes be destroyed.

Without such costumes, Klansmen would be exposed and therefore useless as terrorists. However, the declaration merely served to disassociate Forrest and the KKK leaders from the actions of the thousands of Ghouls with sinister intent. In fact, Klan violence continued to fester. They ignored Forrest's declaration and continued to beat, whip, and murder those brave enough to teach black children, as well as blacks who dared to attempt to live out the American dream. One common target for Klan violence was anyone promoting the Republican cause, because most Republicans had supported the recently assassinated Abraham Lincoln, as well as the post-war policy of Reconstruction, which sought to rebuild the South and incorporate blacks into the political process.

On March 30, 1870, with the enthusiastic backing of President Ulysses S. Grant, the House of Representatives ratified the Fifteenth Amendment that demanded suffrage for all American men regardless of race. The law permitted the federal government to take any necessary steps to ensure that blacks in the South were free to vote. However, Klan intimidation and terror prevented the amendment from truly taking effect; local authorities in states such as Tennessee, Alabama, and Mississippi looked the other way. In 1871, a small group of blacks in Mississippi were placed on trial for allegedly causing civil unrest in their demands to be allowed to vote. As the trial began, other blacks congregated outside the court, which spurred Klansmen to action. They arrived on the scene and shot and killed several blacks. They then grabbed the blacks who had been on trial, dragged them away, and hanged them.

About a year later, the House debated another bill stipulating that any citizen could sue in a federal court any person or persons who had deprived him of rights guaranteed by the Constitution. Among those supporting the bill was Massachusetts Congressman Benjamin Franklin Butler, a former Union Army general who was reviled in the South. Butler read to his fellow House members a letter written by missionary William Luke just before the Alabama Klan had murdered him for his support of Southern blacks. The heartrending note to

Luke's wife, as well as the testimony of hundreds of other victims of the KKK, prompted the House to pass the bill that became known as the Ku Klux Klan Act on April 20, 1871.

Meanwhile, South Carolina governor Robert Scott pleaded for government intervention into his state's Klan problem. President Grant sent troops led by Major Lewis Merrill, who arrived in South Carolina's York County. Merrill (who later returned to the Cavalry and was killed by the Sioux at the Battle of the Little Bighorn in 1876) discovered that about two-thirds of all York County citizens were affiliated with the Klan. He learned that among the most essential Klan tasks were keeping blacks away from the ballot boxes and intimidating and forcing whites who voted for Republican candidates, and therefore for the Reconstruction policies, to renounce their allegiances. Merrill kept government officials apprised of Klan activity in York County, which included six murders, sixty-eight floggings, and five schoolhouse burnings.

Grant then sent U.S. Attorney General Amos Akerman to York County to confirm Merrill's findings that local authorities and juries were either too intimidated by the Klan or too much in favor of its activities to bring justice to Klansmen, not only in that area but throughout South Carolina. Grant acted swiftly, suspending the court system in that state and placing the U.S. Army above local authority. Soon fifty South Carolina Cyclops and other Klan leaders fled South Carolina. Hundreds of others were arrested. Their trials were held in the state capital of Columbia and were well covered by the media. The details of Klan crimes set off a firestorm of indignation and anger nationally and even disgusted native Carolinians. The South Carolina Klan had been crushed by the end of 1871.

The government then dispatched subcommittees to Alabama, Mississippi, Georgia, North Carolina, and Florida. But the court system was overwhelmed by cases against the Klan and simply couldn't keep up. The enforcement policy against the Klan collapsed in 1873. The Congress turned down increased funds for the Justice Department, which signaled the end to Klan prosecution. Southern states therefore passed their own laws, reducing blacks to a subservient role in society. The Jim Crow era had begun. Klan intimidation that kept blacks from the voting booth and frightened whites from voting Republican resulted in Democratic governors being elected in Georgia,

Texas, Alabama, Arkansas, and Mississippi. The Klan had become obsolete due to threats of legal action against them, but states eventually made their efforts unnecessary. Justice fell victim to the will of the majority in the former Confederacy. By the late nineteenth century, government protection for blacks had fallen by the wayside and Supreme Court decisions such as the *Plessy v. Ferguson* "separate but equal" case of 1896 legitimized racial segregation. States began legislating the elimination of black voting through bogus tests, literacy qualifications, and poll taxes and also enacted laws that segregated every public venue from restaurants to beaches to bathrooms to parks. Southern blacks were relegated to menial labor and sent to vastly inferior schools.

Such would be their lot in life, particularly in the South, for another sixty-five years. The Klan would not lie dormant forever; it would be reborn early in the next century and even enjoy widespread acceptance in the South and well beyond. A production created in the earliest days of filmmaking would spur that rebirth.

NOTES

1. Wyn Craig Wade, *The Fiery Cross: The Ku Klux Klan in America* (New York: Simon and Schuster, 1987), 33.
2. Ibid., 34.
3. Reprinted in Walter Fleming, ed., *Documentary History of Reconstruction* (1906; reprint Gloucester, Mass.: Peter Smith, 1960), II: 365.
4. Shelley Klein, *The Most Evil Secret Societies in History* (London: Michael O'Mara Books, 2005), 71.
5. Edward Pollard, Editor, *Richmond Examiner*, as quoted in *New York Tribune*, April 6, 1868.

CHAPTER TWO

Rebirth of the
KKK

The plight of disenfranchised Southern and Northern urban blacks was all but ignored by the turn of the century. Apathy toward their future in America was fueled by a growing belief in black inferiority. An anonymously written book titled *The Negro* even claimed scientific evidence that blacks were animals, not human beings.

Historians began jumping on the bandwagon as well. Several books were written, including one by future president Woodrow Wilson titled *A History of the American People*, glorifying Klansmen as heroes and claiming that the Republican Reconstructionists of the previous generation acted to destroy the South by enfranchising and empowering ignorant and dangerous blacks. The books offered that the Klan was merely acting to preserve and protect the honor of the South and its citizenry. This distortion of history gave fuel to the fire of Southern whites and turned many of their Northern brethren into racists by the early twentieth century.

By that time, however, massive ocean liners were transporting from every corner of the globe millions of new targets for hatred. Immigration began in earnest in the late 1800s. Those who feared competition for jobs or looked for scapegoats for their own miseries or shortcomings displayed an immediate distrust of and prejudice toward foreigners. An estimated 14.5 million immigrants stepped onto American shores from 1900 to 1920, including millions of Catholics. Anti-Catholic sentiment in the United States reached frightening levels. The newly formed American Protective Association was particularly hostile, working to ban Catholics from public office and remove Catholic teachers from public schools.

It was in this environment of racial, ethnic, and religious intolerance that a young filmmaker named D.W. Griffith produced the first celluloid blockbuster in 1915. *Birth of a Nation* was based on a Thomas Dixon novel, *The Clansman*, that was written a decade earlier. The epic grossed an unheard-of $60 million at the box office and not only revolutionized the film industry through its technical achievements and narration, but also triggered a new wave of racism from Maine to California through its portrayal of blacks as little more than barbaric animals bent on attacking and raping white women and the glorification of Klansman as the saviors of the South. The recently formed National Association for the Advancement of Colored People (NAACP) was unsuccessful in its attempt to halt the distribution of the film. The movie's climax was the KKK rescuing the white heroine from certain rape by castrating and lynching her black tormentor. The movie premiered in Los Angeles before a wildly successful run in New York. Lines formed around every theater in which it was shown. Crowds of white patrons who paid a then-outrageous price of two dollars a ticket packed the theater in Atlanta and cheered the hooded vigilantes. An estimated 25 million Americans viewed the film, half of whom had never previously seen a motion picture.

Soon after the Los Angeles premiere, the film was shown to President Wilson in the White House. He responded with unbridled enthusiasm, stating to Dixon and Griffith that "It is like writing history with lightning, and my only regret is that it is all so terribly true."[1] A later showing in Washington to members of the House, Senate, State Department, and media also elicited praise from the audience.

Such exaltation certainly wasn't forthcoming from blacks and liberal whites who protested vehemently in cities such as Pittsburgh, Chicago, Boston, Milwaukee, Spokane, and Portland. But those reactions were mild compared to the KKK fever that swept the nation. Such items as KKK hats and kitchen aprons were manufactured and sold. University of Chicago students even dressed up as Klansmen for a Halloween party.

Griffiths later claimed he fabricated nothing and that the film was a true depiction of life in the South during Reconstruction based on his reading in recent history books. Critics, however, pointed out that those texts glorified the KKK and were wildly racist.

One firm believer of the accuracy of *Birth of a Nation* was Alabaman William Simmons, the son of a struggling physician whose attempt to become a Methodist minister failed. Simmons harbored thoughts about reviving the Klan and the embracing of the film by the American public convinced him the time was ripe and prompted him to take action. He gathered like-minded friends atop Stone Mountain just outside Atlanta on Thanksgiving night in 1915. He read a passage from the Bible, torched a huge cross that lit up the sky, and ushered in the new Knights of the Ku Klux Klan. The cross burning would become a staple of KKK ceremonies for generations thereafter, as well as a fearful sight to enemies of the organization.

The sheer spectacle and timing of the revival quickly attracted 100 new members. Not only did *Birth of a Nation* pique interest, but a murder case in nearby Marietta, Georgia, that same year also made Atlanta a focal point for the rebirth of the Klan, this time with an added anti-Semitic bent. In late April, a fourteen-year-old employee of the Marietta Pencil Company named Mary Phagan was found raped and murdered in the basement of the building. Jewish factory owner Leo Frank was convicted of the crime despite unsubstantial evidence. The governor of Georgia commuted Frank's death sentence to life imprisonment, which set off a firestorm of protest led by openly racist and anti-Semitic U.S. Representative Thomas Watson, who called for Georgians to avenge Phagan's murder. A month later, Frank was whisked away from a prison farm and hanged. It was the first lynching party in American history to use automobiles.

Yet despite rabid anti-black, anti-Jewish, and anti-Catholic sentiment in the United States and specifically in the Deep South, Simmons struggled to lure members into the new KKK. Therefore, he elicited the help of Edward Clarke and Elizabeth Tyler, co-founders of the Southern Publicity Association that had successfully raised funds for such organizations as the Red Cross and Anti-Saloon League, which fought for and later succeeded in ushering in the era of Prohibition. Clarke and Tyler launched and organized propaganda and a campaign that resulted in Klan membership far exceeding its heights during the nineteenth century. Top promoters and organizers were given such colorful titles as Imperial Kleagle and Grand Goblin.

Simmons needed a stronger platform to attract new members. He quickly adopted a more vigilant approach. During one address to Georgia Klansmen, he symbolically extracted a Colt automatic from his pocket and placed it on the table, did the same with a revolver, took out a bowie knife and slammed it between the guns, and said "Now let the niggers, the Catholics, Jews and all who disdain my imperial wizardry come on."[2]

During America's involvement in World War I in 1917 and 1918, Klan membership was centered almost exclusively in the South and Southwest. But the aftermath of World War I forever changed race relations and served to popularize the KKK in the urban north as well due to the intolerance of whites who rebelled against equal opportunities for blacks in the areas of housing, education, and employment. Black soldiers served their country and helped win the war, but returned to the same lack of opportunity that had plagued them before they left. Nearly 1 million blacks had moved north for better treatment during the early part of the century, but were discovering that racism was definitely not exclusive to the South. Anger and tension boiled over, resulting in race riots, including brutal battles between whites and blacks in Chicago, Washington, Knoxville, Omaha, and Tulsa. Most of the insurrections were started by white mobs, although blacks certainly had a greater reason to be in a fighting spirit. In 1919 alone, seventy-four blacks, including veterans, were lynched.

Though Klan responsibility for those murders hasn't been substantiated, it is clear that they were back in the terror business as the Roaring Twenties began. In the fall of 1920, hundreds of Klansmen roamed through Southwestern towns, warning blacks to stay away from the voting booths. A successful black dentist in Houston was murdered by Klansmen who claimed he had been involved with a white woman. In Miami, the archdeacon of a church was stripped and whipped by eight Klansmen for preaching racial equality. Those were just three incidents reported in a landmark investigative report by the *New York World* that ran for two weeks in September 1921. The articles recounted 152 Klan crimes, including four murders, forty-one floggings, and forty-seven tar-and-featherings. The *World* also published an embarrassing story about Clarke and Tyler in which it claimed that in 1919 the two Klan publicists had been caught less than fully dressed and sober in a police raid at a home where questionable sex acts were performed. Though the article stated that the incident cost them only a charge of disorderly conduct and a five-dollar fine, the fact that it came to light at all proved distressing to an organization that was promoting itself as a beacon of morality. But rather than discipline Clarke and Tyler, Klan leaders fired those who called for their dismissal. After all, the two were in the midst of attracting millions of new members.

Meanwhile, the *World* also demanded a complete investigation of the Klan by the U.S. government and got its wish. Simmons was summoned to Washington and promptly claimed that the violent and murderous acts brought forth in the newspaper exposé were the work of imposters. He added that the Klan was not a racist organization, that indeed he had frolicked with black children in his youth, and that his motivation in giving the Klan life once again was both benevolent and fraternal. He went on to say that Catholics, Jews, and blacks were excluded from other clubs and asked why the Klan should be scrutinized and criticized for having the same policy. He defended his fellow Klansmen by pointing out that although they dressed up in ghoulish outfits, so did those attending the Mardi Gras parade.

Simmons was exonerated by his performance. Moreover, the publicity received by the Klan from the *World* articles and the Congressional hearing resulted in a membership explosion. The series increased sales of the *World* by 100,000, but it did far more to popularize the Klan. Simmons claimed that many Klan hopefuls brought with them the Klan exposé clipped from the *World* and other newspapers running the series when they showed up to join the organization. Many from small towns and rural areas joined in part as a way to thumb their noses at the *World* expose, which they considered a prime example of big-city arrogance. Within three months, Clarke reported he was receiving more than 1,000 membership requests daily. In less than a year, Klan membership had catapulted from 100,000 to over a million. Simmons and other Klan members even swore in new president Herbert Hoover in the Green Room of the White House, which gave the organization the ultimate legitimacy.

To attract new members in mainstream America, the Klan shed its outward racist image and embraced religious fundamentalism. They lured in 40,000 evangelical ministers who promoted the KKK from their pulpits throughout the country. The ministers were given free membership in a show of appreciation for their value to the organization. Ministers rose in the Klan to become Grand Cyclopes and even Grand Dragons in Pennsylvania, Texas, North Dakota, and Colorado. The condemnation of the Klan by many at the top of the Protestant and Mormon Church hierarchies had little effect on rank-and-file preachers.

Meanwhile, Klansmen began reading passages from the Bible during their meetings and vowed to serve what they perceived to be the will of God. The calling for a return to a strict religiously-based mindset and lifestyle beckoned millions of Americans who were alarmed by the social changes of the "Roaring Twenties" such as greater promiscuity, lower attendance at church services, and what some considered the overall moral breakdown of society. The famed Scopes Monkey Trial of 1925 that signaled the end of religious teaching in public schools also baited new members to the Klan late during its surge of popularity.

Despite the successful membership drive, disenchantment with William Simmons grew. The Imperial Wizard had become wealthy from Klan expansion while gaining a reputation as a drunkard in an era of Prohibition. Among those who spearheaded a drive to oust Simmons was dentist Hiram Wesley Evans, who headed the Dallas Klavern and was driven by the notion of turning the Klan into a politically oriented organization. Evans was promoted to Imperial Kligrapp (national secretary) and traveled to the thirteen states under his jurisdiction, one of which was Indiana, where a thirty-one-year-old Klansman with political ambitions named David Curtis Stephenson caught his eye. Evans and Stephenson concocted a bold plan to drive Simmons from his post and, indeed, after a bit of chicanery at the 1922 Thanksgiving-week national "Klonvocation," Evans was elected Imperial Wizard and began the politicization process of the KKK in earnest.

The growth of the Klan in mainstream America didn't deter many of its members from using violence. In Waco, Texas, one man was left dead and ten others wounded, including the town sheriff, who was shot twice after he attempted to put a halt to a Klan parade. In Pennsylvania, a black was beaten and hanged. In separate occasions in Denver, Klansmen clubbed a member of the Knights of Columbus and a Jewish attorney with rifle butts. But Evans didn't believe the KKK could make inroads politically through violence. He urged local leaders to keep Klan robes and other garb at the offices to be worn only at meetings and rallies. He even pleaded for local police to become involved in stopping Klan violence, which was curbed drastically under his leadership.

Evans found only moderate success getting Klansmen elected to political offices. Five were voted into the Senate in 1924, including Alabaman Hugo Black, a future Supreme Court judge who quickly became disenchanted with the Klan. But the Klan did take hold in the political situation in Indiana, which was the only state in the country in which every county boasted a Klavern. The rapid growth

Ku Klux Klan in their regalia parade through the streets of Tulsa, Oklahoma, 1923. Note the uniformed police marching alongside the Klansmen. Source: *AP Photo.*

of the KKK in the Hoosier State could be attributed greatly to Stephenson, who played on virulent anti-Catholic sentiment. He even founded a Klan magazine titled *The Fiery Cross*, which became immensely popular. Indiana political figures who spoke out against the Klan were certain to read about supposed gangsterism and prostitution in their cities or counties in the next issue of *The Fiery Cross*.

Stephenson also organized a program in which the Klan researched the background of every candidate who ran for office, from school board to judge to mayor. Aggressive campaigns were staged against all Catholics, blacks, Jews, and anyone else deemed undesirable. Before the 1924 election, the Indiana Klan sent out 250,000 sample ballots to its members, indicating which candidates to vote for. The result was that Klansman Ed Jackson, an unknown before the primary, won the gubernatorial election in 1924 while other KKK members also swept into office.

Soon, however, both Stephenson and the Indiana Klan would be destroyed, as would the image of the organization throughout the country, by the murder of a wholesome young woman named Madge Oberholtzer. The incident would bring about the downfall of the Ku Klux Klan and spell an end to the greatest era of popularity in its history. Oberholtzer was a twenty-eight-year-old who had been an honors student at Butler College before going on to teach at the local public school while doubling as the manager of the Young People's Reading Club. She lived with her parents just two blocks from Stephenson's mansion and had been introduced to him at Jackson's inaugural banquet. She turned back his initial advances, but finally accepted a dinner date. Soon thereafter, she attended a party at Stephenson's home.

On March 15, 1925, she returned home at 9:30 p.m. and was told that Stephenson had been leaving phone messages for her all evening. She was informed that one of his bodyguards, Earl Gentry, would be picking her up shortly. Gentry indeed arrived and walked her to Stephenson's mansion. But Oberholtzer never returned home that night or the following morning, which prompted her parents to contact the police. That afternoon a telegram arrived from Madge indicating that she was in Chicago and would be returning home by train that evening. But her parents waited in vain for her at the station. The following day a stranger knocked on the door and was carrying her in his arms. The man claimed that Oberholtzer, whose entire body was covered with black-and-blue marks, had been in an auto accident, but her testimony to Dr. John Kingsbury told a far more disturbing story. She claimed she had been attacked and beaten in a drawing-room car on a midnight train from Chicago by Stephenson, who was in a drunken frenzy. Then, she added, he literally began eating away at her. She related the following to Kingsbury:

> Stephenson took hold of the bottom of my dress and pulled it up over my head . . . I tried to fight but was weak and unsteady. Stephenson took hold of my two hands and held them. I had not the strength to move. . . . Stephenson took all my clothes off and pushed me into the lower berth. After the train started Stephenson got in with me and attacked me. He held me so I could not move. . . . He chewed all over my body, bit my neck and face, chewing my tongue, chewed my breasts until they bled, my back, my legs, my ankles. . . .[3]

Kidney failure stemming from the beating took Oberholtzer's life less than a month later. Stephenson, who had been arrested for assault and abduction and released on $25,000 bail, was now charged with second-degree murder and placed in jail. Though he claimed he had been framed, the resulting publicity ruined an image of purity and Christian morality the Klan had so laboriously cultivated. As one example, the KKK had vigorously upheld Prohibition in the early 1920s, yet Stephenson had been roaring drunk at the time of the attack.

During his trial, fellow Klansmen encouraged Stephenson by claiming the jury had been fixed in his favor and, even if it judged him guilty, Governor Jackson would certainly pardon him. But Stephenson was indeed convicted of second-degree murder and Jackson did nothing for fear that siding with his KKK buddy would be akin to committing political suicide. Angered by Jackson's refusal to help, the doomed Grand Wizard revealed to the media all the corruption that revolved around the 1924 election, including Indianapolis Mayor John Duvall's signing a document that he would not appoint anybody to the board of public works without Stephenson's consent and Jackson's taking unreported campaign contributions from the KKK. The political careers of both were ruined, as were those of dozens of other Indiana politicians, many of whom landed behind bars.

By the time the investigations slowed to a crawl and the gavels stopped banging, membership in the Indiana Klan had plummeted from 350,000 to a meager 15,000; the national organization had also taken a huge hit. Six hundred Klansmen in New Haven, Connecticut, resigned in one fell swoop and sent a resolution to the Imperial Headquarters that they could no longer remain members and keep their self-respect. The KKK even lost nearly all its members in the Deep South.

Evans responded to the defections by planning a massive show of force in Washington, D.C., in 1925, but only half of the expected 60,000 members showed up. Though it was the largest number of Klansmen ever to congregate for a rally, it was apparent that the incident in Indiana had reversed the organization's wave of popularity that had swept the nation during the previous decade. The Klan had numbered 4 million members in 1924. Six years later, the number had shrunk to 45,000.

The vast majority of the millions of Klansmen who became ex-Klansmen were those who never would have joined the ranks after the Civil War or during the civil rights movement thirty years hence. They were the educated, wealthy, and middle-class whose conservatism and feelings of fraternity rather than hatred of any minority motivated them to swell the Klan membership rolls. That membership would never again rise to significant heights, but KKK brutality had yet to reach its zenith.

NOTES

1. Wyn Craig Wade, *The Fiery Cross: The Ku Klux Klan in America* (New York: Simon and Schuster, 1987), 126.
2. Richard K. Tucker, *The Dragon and the Cross* (Hamden, Conn.: The Shoe String Press, 1991), 24.
3. Ibid., 138.

CHAPTER
THREE The Return of
Terrorism

Scenes of Americans without a care in the world dancing joyously at nightclubs and stories of their fellow countrymen gaining riches on the stock market were replaced by scenes of raggedy unemployed men and women standing in long lines at soup kitchens and stories of hapless folks who had lost everything, including hope.

It was 1930. The Stock Market Crash of 1929 had ushered in the Great Depression. The corporate owners of the landmark film *Birth of a Nation* placed it back in circulation, complete with new soundtrack and sound effects, but public reaction was hardly the same as fifteen years earlier. In fact, virtually nobody showed up aside from Klan recruiters hoping to find new members in a desperate, vain attempt to revitalize the organization. Not only had the illegal activities by the Indiana Klan and the attack and murder of a young woman by its leader in the 1920s proven abhorrent to the general public, but also Americans' preoccupation with the struggles of daily survival was now paramount to giving any thought to the Klan.

What remained of Klan leadership continued in its attempt to play off fear and anger, but blaming Jews or Catholics or blacks for the worst economic crisis in the nation's history wasn't received as a notion with any merit. The Klan then turned its attention to a growing Communist sentiment. Early in 1931, Klansmen whisked away and whipped two Communist organizers in Dallas for publicly espousing racial equality. Although studies showed the fear was unwarranted, the Klan attempted to convince whites that Communists planned to indoctrinate blacks to their cause.

The Klan eventually a found a cause in New Deal legislation created by President Franklin Roosevelt, who took office in 1933. They blamed Jews in the newly formed cabinet such as Secretary of the Treasury Henry Morgenthau for a policy they deemed dangerous to American freedom and also targeted labor unions that were gaining strength during the Roosevelt administration. Imperial Wizard Hiram Wesley Evans, who had remained at his post despite the almost total loss of public support, worked to tie unionism with Communism, but with little success.

Just weeks after Roosevelt moved into the White House, Adolf Hitler and his Nazi Party assumed control of Germany. Naturally, comparisons were made between the philosophies and tactics of the KKK and Nazis. In fact, Rev. Otto Strohschein, a former American Klansmen who moved to Germany in 1923, started a Klan Klavern there that eventually grew to 300 members. Two years later, as Nazism gained popularity in Germany, those in the media who agreed with its principles wrote glowingly about the KKK in the United States. Included was the following excerpt from an editorial in *Hammer Magazine* based in Leipzig:

> May these American reports tend to encourage many German minds; may they be valuable as evidence that the Nordic people in all parts of the world are arousing themselves, and consider themselves on a holy mission; to be a guardian of the spirit of truth and the highest human ideals. . . . If the Klan fulfills its task, it will necessarily reach out its hand over the borderlands with a similar endeavor, to a realization of mutual aims. Then as the cunning enemy of people is united internationally, we will also need a worldwide confederacy of the Nordic races in order to shatter the bonds in which the Jewish offender has smitten all honorable nations.[1]

The feelings of those of Nazi sentiment toward the KKK were mutual. Klansmen in areas with large Jewish populations, particularly in New York, praised Hitler for his anti-Semitism and the programs he was initiating in Germany such as boycotts of Jewish stores. In fact, American Nazi Party leader Fritz Kuhn attempted to merge his organization with the Ku Klux Klan, but the talks ended in 1939 when he was convicted for embezzlement and sent to jail. Replacement G. William Kunze organized a joint rally of Nazis and Klansmen in the summer of 1940, which motivated alarmed congressmen to form a committee to investigate what they considered to be a dangerous linking of right-wing extremists. In the end it didn't matter because the American Nazi Party was forced to disintegrate when the United States entered World War II.

The Klan was poorly run and virtually ignored during the war. Imperial Wizard James Colescott, who took pride in being the first Klansmen to reach that office by coming up through the ranks, announced after the bombing of Pearl Harbor that he was withdrawing from circulation all Klan literature deemed controversial. But in 1942, Klan editors organized dozens of anti-Semitic essays written by auto industry giant Henry Ford into a book, *The International Jew*. The book became a hit in Nazi Germany, much to the anger and embarrassment of Ford, who had recanted his anti-Semitism years earlier. Ford threatened the Klan with legal action if the book wasn't withdrawn from circulation. The result was a thorough investigation of the Klan. And in the spring of 1944, the Internal Revenue Service informed Colescott that the KKK owed $685,000 in back taxes. The Klan was forced to sell all their assets and hand over the proceeds to the U.S. government, but still couldn't pay off the debt, which spelled doom. Colescott called a special meeting that April and asked that the organization be disbanded. He spoke bitterly, blaming "that nigger-loving Roosevelt and that Jew Morgenthau who was his Secretary of the Treasury" for the demise of the Klan.[2]

Several local Klan organizations remained active in the South, particularly in Georgia, where every county boasted a Klavern. A year after the war ended, with news of a Holocaust perpetrated by the German Nazis that claimed 6 million Jewish lives fresh in their minds, three hundred new Klansmen were sworn in during a ceremony at Stone Mountain. Many of the recruits were lawmen and judges from nearby Atlanta. Georgia Klan leader Dr. Samuel Green was soon claiming that the organization was not only beginning to thrive in the South, but also in densely populated northern and western states such as California, New York, Ohio, and New Jersey. But several states, including California and New York, took measures to ban the KKK within their boundaries.

Indeed, the Klan flourished only in the South during the postwar era. Although small in numbers and stature, it proved to be as brutal as ever. Lynching of blacks became commonplace, as did intimidation in the political process. In black communities throughout Georgia, Klansmen backing fellow member Herman Talmadge for governor placed miniature coffins on the porches of citizens and slid warnings in their mailboxes to stay away from the polls. The tactic worked—Talmadge was voted into office.

By the late 1940s, many Americans even in the racist South had grown disgusted with Klan violence. But hardcore racists had taken over in some areas, leading the editor of a tiny black newspaper in North Carolina to write,

> We welcome the Ku Klux Klan to North Carolina, because if it is active it will focus the attention of decent citizens on how asinine, vicious and low in the scale of human depravity some people can descend. . . . It will bring about a choosing of sides between that element of white people who believe in giving the Negro full rights of citizenship and those who do not.[3]

The lines were being drawn in 1949, particularly by renegade Klansmen who created independent groups in Georgia, Alabama, Florida, Tennessee, and the Carolinas. A spate of violence in the Deep South wasn't merely directed at blacks, but also at anyone deemed an enemy of the Klan, including newspaper editors and lawyers. Those who the Klan deemed had displayed even the slightest indiscretions were punished. A group of Klansmen in Tennessee battered two Chattanooga men who refused to kneel in tribute to a burning cross. The Klan beat six others who were sitting in church and had left their families at home. Police officers in Georgia turned over a group of drunken blacks to the Klan for an aggressive flogging. The sheriff in one Georgia town explained that he couldn't investigate the flogging of four men because he had been babysitting. The newly formed Federated Ku Klux Klans of Alabama took action when

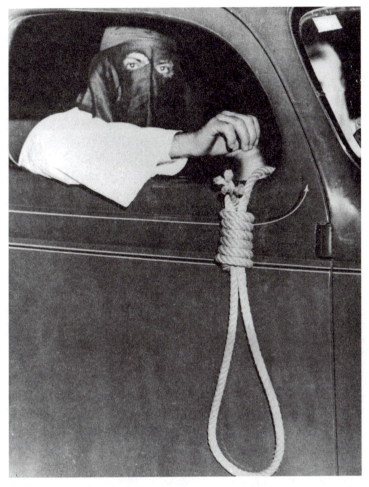

A hangman's noose dangling from an automobile driven by a hooded Ku Klux Klan member was among the grim warnings to blacks to stay away from the voting places in a municipal primary election in Miami, Florida, 1939. In spite of the threats, 616 blacks exercised their right to vote. Source: *AP Photo.*

learning that a woman allowed high school students to use her home for what was believed to be sexual activity. Klansmen dragged her from her house and threatened to burn her at the stake. Fellow Klansmen from the same group flogged a woman for encouraging a boy the Klan didn't approve of to date her daughter. The Klan also trashed a café that the owner had decided to integrate.

The Georgia Klan proved particularly violent and indiscriminate. A series of floggings rocked that state in 1949 and 1950. Individuals who Klansmen decided drank too much, failed to take care of their families, engaged in immoral cohabitation, or were even deemed too lazy were candidates to be dragged from their homes and flogged. Most of the victims were white.

The result of the increase in Klan violence during that era was that anti-mask laws were being debated in many states and passed in some. Even Georgia governor Herman Talmadge, who had won the 1948 election greatly through Klan support, was forced to sign a bill that made it illegal for Klansmen to wear their masks in public. A similar bill was pushed through in Florida and South Carolina, which also prohibited intimidating cross burnings.

Two little mascots, equipped with their own robes and hoods, flank Dr. Samuel Green, Ku Klux Klan Grand Dragon, in Atlanta, Georgia, 1948, during a massive initiation ceremony of 700 members of the Ku Klux Klan. Source: *AP Photo.*

The death of Imperial Wizard Samuel Green in 1949 heralded the emergence of other leaders, including Green disciple Tom Hamilton, who greatly influenced Klansmen in Georgia and North Carolina. He was eventually named Grand Dragon of North Carolina, where he thrived despite the concerted efforts of the FBI, local officials, and newspaper editorial campaigns. Hamilton boasted his Klan was unstoppable and he appeared to be right until 1952, when a group of his Klansmen pulled an unmarried couple out of bed, dragged them across the state line to South Carolina, and tortured them. The FBI became involved in the resulting court case, from which more than a dozen Klansmen were found guilty and imprisoned. Included in that group was Hamilton, who spent four years behind bars.

Although individual Klansmen still operated throughout the South, the organization itself was barely breathing by the early 1950s; however, a Supreme Court ruling in 1954 gave the Klan a cause to rally around. The Court determined in *Brown v. Board of Education* that the separate-but-equal policies of the South were inherently unequal and voted to strike down school segregation. Southern states simply ignored the ruling, which prompted the Court to order in 1955 that districts practicing segregation must integrate "with all deliberate speed." That vague wording allowed those in charge of Southern schools to further dawdle with their implementation and gave the KKK an opportunity to gain membership and step up violence against blacks.

By 1957, the KKK numbered about 40,000, the vast majority of whom were racist, violent thugs who preyed on their perceived enemies, particularly blacks. The civil rights movement had begun, and though most blacks followed the lead of Dr. Martin Luther King, Jr., a twenty-seven-year-old minister who eschewed violence, others had become angry enough and had gained enough courage to fight back. Robert Williams, a black war veteran and former marine, successfully integrated the library in Monroe, North Carolina, before setting his sights on swimming pools, restaurants, and other public places. The KKK responded by terrorizing the local black community, which motivated Williams to apply for and receive a charter from the National Rifle Association. He trained his friends how to use firearms. And in the summer of 1957, hooded Klansmen drove down his street, honking their horns, and bellowing out threats along the way.

They were stunned to see Williams and other blacks shooting at them with their rifles. The Klansmen, who were not their equals in marksmanship, hightailed it out of the area quickly.

King launched his campaign with a bus boycott in Montgomery, Alabama, where blacks had been forced to sit in the back of the buses. Official integration of Montgomery buses a year later proved to be the first in a long line of triumphs for King and other Southern blacks. It also served to increase Klan membership, but Klansmen throughout the South did more bickering among themselves than they did uniting for a single purpose. The result was mindless, vicious violence by rogue Klansmen. In one particularly cruel display, Alabama Klansmen ritualistically abducted black handyman Edward Aaron, castrated him with razor blades, then poured kerosene and turpentine over his wounds.

Nothing, however, could stop the civil rights movement begun by King. In Greensboro, North Carolina, a group of empowered black teenagers plopped down at the integrated Woolworth's lunch counter and demanded to be served. The tactic gained favor among blacks through the South. Soon sixty-eight Southern cities became hotbeds of such protests, which were organized by such groups as the Congress of Racial Equality (CORE) and the Student Nonviolent Coordinating Committee (SNCC). Klansmen and other racist Southerners began decrying the tactics not only of blacks to force integration, but also of white northerners who they claimed were Communists and believed to be stirring up trouble as well.

One of the most publicized instances of Klan violence occurred in 1958 when CORE-organized "freedom riders" consisting of six whites and seven blacks were bused to several Southern cities in an effort to achieve integration at bus terminals. Included were trips to New Orleans and the Alabama cities of Anniston and Montgomery, where groups of Klansmen were ready for them the moment they descended from the bus. Klansmen who had been given free rein beat the freedom riders unmercifully. The Birmingham police, led by notorious Bull Connor, had told fellow Klansmen they would be given fifteen minutes "to beat them, bomb them, burn them, shoot them, do anything (they) wanted to with absolutely no intervention whatsoever by the police."[4]

In the early 1960s, various Klan splinter groups united and formed the United Klans of America (UKA), which was led by former Alabama KKK head Robert Shelton. The unabashedly racist Shelton, who showed up to meetings along with several henchmen in full military garb, was named Imperial Wizard of the merged organizations. The UKA sought to disrupt or kill all integration efforts. Among the most publicized examples was that perpetrated against black Air Force veteran James Meredith, who applied for admission into segregated University of Mississippi. When he arrived on campus, he and federal marshal escorts were greeted by hundreds of angry white students and dozens of gun-toting and rock-throwing Klansmen and other protesters. By the end of that hectic evening, two people, including a French reporter, lay dead. Soon thereafter, President John F. Kennedy sent 3,000 troops and National Guardsmen to the school to ensure Meredith's admission. A similar violent protest took place at the University of Alabama, where angry white students and Klansmen listened with satisfaction as notoriously racist governor and Klan hero George Wallace refused admission to two black students.

The incidents on the two Southern college campuses infuriated many Americans, though others believed individual states had the right to fight integration of their schools. But in mid-September 1963, another violent act perpetrated by the Klan raised their ire to a fever pitch—the bombing of a black church in Birmingham that killed four young black girls who were inside the church. Hardened Klansman Robert E. Chambliss, who prided himself in his working knowledge of explosives, was charged with the murders, but was acquitted by an all-white jury. It wasn't until 1977 that a retrial brought Chambliss to justice and sent him to jail, where he eventually died.

The church bombing was followed by an incident in St. Augustine, Florida. The nation's oldest city became a war zone when dentist and black activist Dr. Robert Hayling began working for racial equality. That motivated area Klansman Reverend Charles Conley Lynch to call for a massive Klan rally at a clearing in the nearby woods. In his speech, he railed against Jews and blacks and claimed that those who perpetrated the church bombing should have medals pinned to their chests. He insisted that the goal of the Klan should be to exterminate all blacks, and he had a few choice words about Hayling.

An unidentified Klansman passes out handbills to supporters standing in front of a hotel in Atlanta, Georgia, July 4, 1962. The KKK handed out the bills after members of the NAACP began picketing hotels, motels, and eating establishments in protest of their segregation policies. The picketer in the foreground, a student at the University of Michigan, holds a sign urging integration at Atlanta hotels. Source: *AP Photo/Horace Court.*

"You've got a nigger in St. Augustine ought not to live," he exclaimed to his fellow Klansmen, "that burr-headed bastard of a dentist. He's got no right to live at all, let alone breathe the white man's free air. He ought to wake up tomorrow morning with a bullet between his eyes. If you were half the men you claim to be, you'd kill him before sunup." And when Hayling and three other black men were seen spying on the rally, the Klansmen, who had been worked in a frenzy by Lynch, now had a cause to take action. One white-robed woman shouted, "Castrate the bastards! Knock their heads off! Kill them, kill them! They had to trespass to get here; they've got no right to live! Come on, do something! String them up!"[5]

Both male and female Klansmen, in a fever pitch, beat Hayling with fists, clubs, and gun butts. His life was saved by Irvin Chaney, a white man representing the Florida Council on Human Relations, who had been watching from afar with curiosity and was overwhelmed by the ferocity and viciousness of the attack. Suspecting that local law enforcement officers would look the other way, Chaney contacted the FBI and the Florida adjutant general's office. They sped to the scene and broke up the attack just as Klansmen were preparing to pour kerosene on Hayling and his associates. But, as usual, the Klansmen were acquitted of all charges.

The free rein given to the KKK in many Southern communities resulted in many more deaths in the mid-1960s. Among those to fall was army officer Lemuel Penn, who was driving innocently to Washington, D.C., after a training period at Fort Benning, Georgia. Klansmen spotted a car with a black driver and black passengers and a Washington license plate, which led them to believe they were civil rights workers. They proceeded to gun down Penn. And in the subsequent trial, the Klansmen walked away with a not guilty verdict handed down by an all-white jury.

Such injustices spurred more Northerners with strong consciences to take action. Among them were Jewish activists Andrew Goodman and Michael "Mickey" Schwerner, who as members of the fledgling Council of Federated Organizations (COFO) had been sent to Meridian, Mississippi, to fight for civil rights, including the right to vote. The two elicited the help of twenty-one-year-old black Meridian native James Chaney. Mississippi was considered a hotbed of Klan activity and arguably the most racist state in the country. During World War II, when asked what punishment Hitler should receive for his crimes if captured alive, one black soldier suggested that the German dictator be painted black and dropped into the heart of Mississippi. The brutality of the Klan in that state was heightened when violently racist businessman Samuel Bowers was selected as its Imperial Wizard.

Bowers warned his constituents in 1964 that a battle between what he perceived to be Northern Carpetbaggers and the Southern way of life was going to be waged that summer. The Meridian Klan was particularly aware of Schwerner's activities and planned on murdering him. In fact, the method of killing was a main topic of conversation at a Mississippi Klan meeting in mid-June. Several days later, the Neshoba County deputy sheriff arrested Chaney on a trumped-up charge of speeding and locked him up, as well as passengers Schwerner and Goodman. After paying a fine, the trio sped off in a Ford station wagon. But they didn't travel far. In fact, they were never seen again. Their disappearance triggered a massive investigation in which the FBI successfully interviewed 1,000 white southerners, including 488 Klansmen. A month and a half later, the remains of the missing civil rights workers were found in an earthen dam. That December, six Klansmen were charged with conspiring to violate the civil rights of the three COFO workers, but those who knew how they were killed refused to talk. It wasn't until October 1967 that enough evidence had been gathered through paid informants and other intrigue to bring the case to trial. U.S. Assistant Attorney John Doar explained what had happened to the civil rights workers:

> After they were released about ten-thirty from custody, they were chased down by three cars, one of which was driven by Cecil Price, deputy sheriff, in an official state law car, and as they got fifteen or sixteen miles south of (the nearby town of Philadelphia), they were stopped on a side road, and again placed in custody of Price. . . . They were taken in Price's car, four or five miles back up toward Philadelphia in Neshoba County. The deputy sheriff turned off the side road, stopped his car. The boys were taken out of the car and shot at close, contact range.[6]

According to defendant Horace Barnette, fellow Klansman James Jordan expressed frustration that he didn't have an opportunity to shoot Goodman or Schwerner. Barnette recalled Jordan exclaiming, "You didn't leave me anything but a nigger" before he shot and killed Chaney.[7]

But times were beginning to change in the South. Whereas previous trials against Klansmen resulted in not-guilty verdicts handed down by all-white juries, this time Price and Bowers were sent to jail. The anger over such brutal incidents resonating from all over the country was beginning to make a dent in the actions taken by violent racists. One such episode revolved around Detroit housewife Viola Liuzzo, who spent much of her earlier life in Georgia and rural Tennessee and whose conscience was stirred by the mistreatment of blacks in the South, particularly during the infamous beatings of blacks fighting for the right to vote by lawmen in Selma, Alabama, in 1965. Among those who were killed by Klansmen was Reverend James Reeb, a Unitarian minister from Boston who was battered by clubs and lead pipes and died two days later.

Television coverage of the incident motivated Liuzzo to travel to Selma to join a march to Montgomery organized by King to draw attention to black voting rights. The march went peacefully for Liuzzo, but as she planned to return to Michigan, Klansmen spotted her driving alongside a black teenager from Selma named LeRoy Moton, who was involved in the movement. Seconds later, shots rung out and Liuzzo was dead from gunshot wounds to the head. Moton survived by passing out. Three Klansmen were indicted for the murder.

Despite overwhelming evidence against the Klansmen, the first trial resulted in a hung jury and the second found them not guilty. The federal government was again forced to take action, charging the Klansmen with violating the civil rights of Liuzzo and Moton. They were finally found guilty and sentenced to ten years in jail, though many believed that Leroy Wilkins, who pulled the trigger, should have received a life sentence.

The party was over for the Klan by the late 1960s. Klansmen could no longer hope for the widespread support that they had enjoyed in the early 1920s. Although they could no longer count on impunity for the crimes they committed, the Klan was far from dead. New civil rights issues prompted more violent action as the seventies approached.

NOTES

1. Wyn Craig Wade, *The Fiery Cross: The Ku Klux Klan in America* (New York: Simon and Schuster, 1987), 267.
2. Stetson Kennedy, *I Rode with the Ku Klux Klan* (London: Arco Publishing, 1954), 221.

3. Alva W. Taylor, "Klan Seen Trying for a Comeback," *Christian Century* 67 (February 1, 1950): 150.

4. Carl M. Brauer, *John F. Kennedy and the Second Reconstruction* (New York: Columbia University Press, 1977), 98–109.

5. Ibid., 327.

6. Patsy Sims, *The Klan* (Lexington, Ky.: The University Press of Kentucky, 1996), 216–217.

7. Ibid., 217.

| # Kleaner Klan

America had shifted to the left politically by the early 1970s. Tired and disgusted by the seemingly never-ending war in Vietnam and influenced by a society more accepting of different cultures, the huge majority of Americans viewed the KKK as nothing more than a small, radically violent group that attempted unsuccessfully to prevent blacks from gaining their rightful place in society.

Laws such as the Civil Rights Act and Voting Rights Act stripped away the last vestiges of Jim Crow in the South, where racial relations had become more tolerant and views of civil rights had begun to change. In 1974, the FBI estimated that Klan membership had dwindled to an all-time low of about 1,500. It even appeared that the organization was threatened with extinction.

Klan leaders harkened back to the only era in which the KKK had earned wide acceptance for its future strategy. The group had gained popularity for a decade after the launching of the film *Birth of a Nation* by espousing Christian morality and eschewing violence, at least outwardly. They accepted that the Klansmen could never regain a foothold in America if they continued to fuel their image as terrorists. So some leaders replaced their hoods and robes with suits and ties in an attempt at legitimization.

The new "Klean Klan" played on the reaction to controversial new issues in race relations to gain favor. Among them was affirmative action, which gave blacks preferential treatment in the hiring process to reverse past discrimination. Another was court-ordered busing of inner-city black children to white suburban schools and vice versa, which forced integration in an attempt to provide an equal education for all. The Klan made inroads capitalizing on white rage over both issues in the early 1970s. And in 1974, the White Knights of the Ku Klux Klan named a new Imperial Wizard who would play the lead role in transforming its image.

That man was David Duke, who understood that the Klan could never garner sympathy in modern America nor make an impact politically by lynching blacks, burning crosses, and spewing out hateful rhetoric during rallies in the backwoods of rural Southern towns. He preferred to be referred to as "National Director" rather than "Imperial Wizard" and spoke only in veiled terms of anti-Semitism and perceived black inferiority and in glowing terms of his love for the white race, which he claimed was losing its rights in the areas of employment and education.

Duke presented himself like a slick billboard advertisement for the Klan. Tall, handsome, outgoing, and charismatic, he attempted to give racism a friendly face. The native Oklahoman belied the image of the ignorant Klansman. He graduated from Louisiana State University in 1974 with a degree in history, though his specific areas of study included white supremacy, anti-Semitism, and Nazism. His goal was to recruit college students, white intellectuals, and even Catholics. He professed non-violence and never used racial and ethnic slurs such as "nigger" or "kike" in public, greatly because he believed that convincing others that he was striving for the benefit of the white race rather than the downfall of traditional Klan enemies was a key to its future success.

Duke lost a campaign for a seat in the Louisiana Senate in 1975 before embarking on several unsuccessful runs at a United States Senate seat, Governor of Louisiana, and even the Presidency in the late 1980s and 1990s. But the fact that he nearly won the governorship in 1991 suggests not only that the South had yet to divorce itself from its racist ties, but also that Duke still enjoyed a great deal of magnetism two decades after bursting onto the scene.

One of Duke's disciples was Louis Beam, who was appointed Grand Dragon in Texas. A Vietnam War veteran who spoke incessantly about his experiences of killing during the war and his anticipation of more killing during an inevitable race war, Beam was among the first survivalists. He lured Klansmen from throughout the country to train with him at one of several military-style bases he created in the state. While Duke spoke calmly and intelligently in public, Beam ranted. "I've got news for you, nigger," he raved at a rally. "I'm not going to be in front of my television set, I'm going to be hunting you. I've got the Bible in one hand and a .38 in the other hand and I know what to do."[1]

Another Duke disciple was Tom Metzger, a native Indianan and one-time leader of the White Brotherhood who was named the Grand Dragon in California. Another Duke appointee was Bill Wilkinson, whom he chose as the new Dragon in his home state of Louisiana. Wilkinson fit the desired mold, having graduated from high school at age sixteen. Following a stint in the navy, he moved to California, where he became disgusted at the sight of inter-racial couples and developed into an avowed racist. Attracted by Duke's new intellectual approach, he immediately took an offer to become leader of the Louisiana Klan.

Duke, however, quickly alienated his fellow White Knights for what they believed to be his self-promotion, particularly during a tour of London in the spring of 1978 that so angered the citizenry that the British Home Secretary signed an order of deportation. By that time, Metzger had already become entrenched with the United Klans of America while Wilkinson had begun to take over Klan leadership with more openly violent tactics. Wilkinson made a name for himself during the presidential elections of 1976 when he showed up at a Baptist Church service attended by Democratic candidate Jimmy Carter, donned his KKK robe, and had his picture taken in front of the building. Two years later, Wilkinson was calling for revolt against blacks while traveling and posing for photographers with a small cache of guns. He bragged that the guns were for killing people and that the Klan intended to use bullets and bombs and not books to fight its battles.

Wilkinson also spearheaded a recruiting drive in the American armed services. After a fight broke out between white and black marines at Camp Pendleton in 1976, contraband such as a .357 magnum, clubs, knives, and KKK literature and a membership list were uncovered on the premises. By late that decade, Klan activity in all branches of the military had grown at an alarming rate and, in fact, a cross-burning ceremony even took place on the mess deck of the aircraft carrier *America*.

Another group with which Wilkinson made inroads was Vietnam veterans, many of whom became particularly angry in 1979, when President Carter pardoned draft dodgers who had been living in Canada and invited them to return home. Veterans who believed blacks had been given preferential treatment in the United States via affirmative action and other programs intended to right past discriminatory hiring practices began joining the Klan.

The result of Wilkinson's efforts was that Klan membership skyrocketed 25 percent from March 1978 through the end of the decade. Buoyed by his own success, he spurred his members to acts of violence. In February 1979, Klansmen responded to demonstrations by blacks in Decatur, Alabama, who were protesting the conviction of a severely retarded black man who had been accused of raping three white women despite tests indicating he didn't boast the motor skills to drive a car that was a key piece of evidence in the trial. Wilkinson organized 150 Klansmen to drive through the area as they brandished shotguns and pistols. The civil rights organization Southern Christian Leadership Conference held a march in late May, but they were met by a group of armed Klansmen. Decatur police attempted to clear a path for the demonstrators by moving out the Klansmen, who ran to their cars, pulled out guns, and began shooting. When the last of about 20 shots had been fired, three black marchers and two Klansmen had been hit, though none of them had been fatally wounded.

Victims of Klan violence wouldn't be so lucky on November 3, 1979. The members of the Communist Worker's Party (CWP) in October had been granted a permit to stage a "Death to the Klan" rally in Greensboro, North Carolina. The CWP was unaware, however, that the Greensboro police force included an enthusiastic KKK member named Edward Dawson, who had served nine months in prison a decade earlier for his role in the murder of a local black girl. Dawson began recruiting Klansmen for the rally, which featured about fifty CWP members. The CWP had provoked the Klan by inviting White Knights leader Joe Grady to attend and face the wrath of the people. Rival Klan leader Virgil Griffin decided, however, he would be there. His group formed an alliance with local Nazis and was not about to allow the CWP to denounce them publicly as cowards, as they feared when Grady declined the invitation to attend. Meanwhile, the CWP had provided the police with its parade route, which gave them permission to march. A Klan request to be given a copy of the parade route document was granted by a city attorney, who ruled it was public knowledge.

The rally never had a chance to get started. About an hour before it was scheduled to begin, about thirty Nazis and Klansmen arrived on the scene, including several with weapons. Then several cars containing Griffin's Klansmen and neo-Nazis pulled up, whereupon CWP members raced over and began pummeling those in the lead car, which included Dawson. The Klansmen stopped their cars, walked to their trunks, pulled out rifles and handguns and begin shooting at the demonstrators, whom they knew were unarmed. In a matter of a minute and a half five protesters lay dead or dying, while eight others were wounded. The Klansmen then placed their weapons back in their trunks and drove off. Despite the fact that President Carter ordered the FBI to investigate the shootings, only sixteen of the forty Klansmen and Nazis were arrested, and just four of the former and two of the latter were brought to trial. Conspiracy charges were dropped, much to the dismay of the victims' families. Defense attorneys claimed the CWP triggered the violence and that the Klansmen and neo-Nazis had reacted in self-defense. The jury agreed and acquitted all the defendants.

The Klan had killed five Communists with immunity, which motivated Wilkinson to step up his membership drive. In the late 1970s, the United States economy was struggling, and Iranian students had taken Americans hostage. Wilkinson blamed integration for what he perceived to be the nation's drop into second-class status. The country experienced a general shift to the right and a rebirth of fundamentalist Christian fervor. That pushed some far enough to the right to embrace Klan philosophies, though most church members were embarrassed and disgusted when Klansmen began joining their congregations. Klan membership continued to grow into the early 1980s as Wilkinson took advantage of the old tactic of finding and exploiting racial problems anywhere in the country. He drove to Idabel, Oklahoma, in January 1980 after a young black man had been shot behind a nightclub deemed for whites only and proclaimed that a Klavern would shortly be open for business in that area. He held a large Klan rally in Mississippi after policemen killed a pregnant black woman in Jackson. He organized another demonstration in Uniontown, Pennsylvania, where unemployed coal mine workers deemed affirmative action was to blame for their problems.

By that time, Klan leaders were falling all over themselves to take the lead in turning the KKK into a military organization. Texas Grand Dragon Louis Beam was allowing his disciples, including several Vietnam veterans with experience in firearms, to use various weapons in four military camps in that state. Wilkinson, meanwhile, unveiled Camp My Lai, in Alabama. That military camp was named after the Vietnamese village in which the massacre of the entire population by U.S. soldiers during the war caused great controversy. Wilkinson even ran a summer camp for children, who received training in Klan philosophy and the use of various weapons, then were sent out to shopping malls and their own schools with racist and anti-Semitic literature in an attempt to recruit more members. The kids didn't just learn about the Klan—they took action. One group in Decatur torched gasoline-soaked school buses to protest busing, and another in Oklahoma beat gays with a baseball bat. Near Houston, a Klansman trained ten teenagers in the use of firearms and in hand-to-hand combat, which included the nuances of slicing off a head with a machete.

The unbridled violence taught by the Klan resulted in a spate of attacks in the early 1980s. Three Chattanooga Klansmen shot five black women, four of whom were merely walking down the street while the other was planting flowers in front of her home. Black rioting resulted from the acquittal of two of the Klansmen and minor charges meted out to the other. Even more random was the murder of Michael Donald, a nineteen-year-old black from Mobile, Alabama, who was whisked away by Klansmen, strangled, and hung from a tree. The Klansmen admitted they had never met Donald, but that their intention was to show Klan strength in that state. That murder resulted in the first sentence dooming a Klansman to the electric chair; however, it took a federal court judge to make that pronouncement.

Klansmen were also arrested in Baltimore for planning to bomb the local office of the NAACP and in New Jersey for shooting into the home of a black family. The increasing number of blacks moving into previously all-white middle-class neighborhoods in the 1980s proved alarming to many whites and provided tremendous motivation for Klan violence.

Despite it all, Klan membership soared, which proved to the proud Wilkinson that the violent tactics under his regime were far more attractive to potential recruits than the intellectual approach to further the cause espoused by Duke, who left the Klan in the early 1980s to launch an organization called the National Association for the Advancement of White People. Duke soon discovered that without the robes and the hoods, the burning crosses, and the possibility of smashing a few skulls, few were interested. The new organization, which claimed it supported white separatism rather than white supremacy, failed to attract members and remained a nonentity.

Klan violence in the early 1980s, however, did cause a backlash. Klansmen were met with highly charged counterdemonstrations at their rallies while the National Educational Association (NEA) and American Federation of Teachers (AFT) also became involved, increasing their efforts to provide students with anti-Klan literature and lectures. The NEA proposed openly discussing Klan violence and the notion of white supremacy in classrooms, which its leaders believed would end the mystic attraction that led some youth to the KKK.

But it was groups such as the Anti-Defamation League (ADL), Southern Christian Leadership Conference (SCLC) and Southern Poverty Law Center (SPLC) that stepped forward to stem the tide of Klan expansion. In fact, about thirty civil rights organizations formed the National Anti-Klan Network, which researched and monitored Klan violence throughout the country. The SPLC was particularly vigilant. It formed the Klanwatch Project, which was critical of the Justice Department and the Reagan Administration for what it felt was a lax attitude toward KKK activity, so it took matters into its own hands by taking the Klan to court. In the process of representing immigrant Vietnamese fishermen in Texas who had been terrorized by the Klan, the SPLC discovered an obscure law that forbade private armies in that state. The judge ruled that the military training school run by Beam and his henchmen had to be closed, which so infuriated Beam that he abandoned the Texas Klan altogether.

Other lawsuits followed, including one for victims of Klan violence in Decatur, Illinois, in which Klanwatch asked for $43 million

Members of the Ku Klux Klan salute at a gathering for the third Annual Hico KKK Rally in Hico, Texas, 1992. Source: *AP Photo/Pat Sullivan.*

in damages. Wilkinson began pleading with members for funds to fight the legal battles, but the task was overwhelming. More moderate members didn't believe it was their responsibility to pay for the extreme violence perpetrated by others and began leaving the organization in droves, which prompted Wilkinson to file for bankruptcy and take violent measures against Klanwatch. In the summer of 1983, Klansmen broke into the SPLC and firebombed the offices of Klanwatch, but that merely served to embolden the efforts of the organization. In fact, donations from throughout the country helped build a new fireproof and bombproof building and the Klansmen responsible for the action were sent to jail. Soon thereafter, the Decatur case came to a head with the imprisonment of four Alabama Klan leaders, including the Grand Dragon and Exalted Cyclops.

That was the straw that broke Wilkinson's back. He resigned as Imperial Wizard and left the Klan. By that time, splinter groups such as the Aryan Nations were attracting and militarizing American right-wing radicals, including former Klansmen, neo-Nazis, and young racists such as skinheads. By the 1990s, the Klan had shrunk to an estimated 5,000 to 8,000 members, two-thirds of whom resided in the South, and had been broken into several chapters. Five members of the Imperial Klans of America were charged with murdering a sixteen-year-old Hispanic boy at a Kentucky county fair in 2005 and ordered to pay $2.5 million in damages. But such incidents were few and far between. The Klan was seen as an organization out-of-step with racist youth, many of whom were touting a race war to bring what they believed to be an inevitable confrontation between blacks and whites to a head.

NOTE

1. Wyn Craig Wade, *The Fiery Cross: The Ku Klux Klan in America* (New York: Simon and Schuster, 1987), 373.

The Klan
Philosophy

Nearly 150 years have passed. The Industrial Revolution came and went. Five major wars were fought. The inventions of radio, television, and computers drastically altered our ability to communicate. The advent of automobiles and airplanes sent Americans places they had only dreamed of visiting. Man even walked on the moon. Yet through it all, the Ku Klux Klan has steadfastly embraced the same philosophy about race relations that it did during the period of Reconstruction that followed the Civil War. The accepted view is that the philosophy that drives the Klan is based on ignorance and fueled by bitterness, anger, and fear.

Each era has presented different circumstances that have given Klansmen what they perceive as justification to feel such emotion, as well as a strategy to elicit strength in numbers. Before the turn of the nineteenth century, the freedom and enfranchisement of blacks brought on fear in the South that they would take away jobs from whites and vote fellow blacks into office. White backlash also arose at the notion of integration. The degree of mistrust and anger felt by many whites allowed Klansmen to literally get away with murder. Following the release of *Birth of a Nation* in 1915, Klansmen used the increasing public belief in black inferiority and played off growing resentment over competition for jobs provided by mass immigration to gain support. The Klan used supposed Christian morality and toned down violence to attract millions to its cause. But when the civil rights movement began in the 1950s, the Klan showed little interest in a mass membership drive. The immediacy of the threat to segregation motivated Klansmen to take violent action, resulting in lynchings and bombings that cost hundreds of lives of blacks and civil rights workers. They were driven by their philosophy of white supremacy and what they saw as a deterioration of society through integration. A decade later, prompted by a public sickened by such violence, Klansmen such as David Duke attempted to gain support politically while playing off white anger over such issues as busing and affirmative action.

But throughout those 150 years, the overriding force pushing the Klan to action was the belief in inherent white superiority and the dangers of any black influence on society. White supremacists, motivated by the belief that there are actual physical differences in the blood of Africans and African Americans, point to the lack of technological advancement in African societies and claim that blacks don't boast the same capabilities as whites. They overlook the achievements of African communities, particularly when those achievements are motivated more by spirituality and tradition rather than by industrial or capitalistic goals. They also ignore the societal advancements achieved by American blacks who have been given opportunities, which has resulted in a huge increase in the black middle and upper classes and even the first black president in 2008.

Both the epic film *Birth of a Nation* and the philosophy of the second-era KKK was based on the 1905 Thomas Dixon book, *The Clansman*. The work glorified the "Invisible Empire" during the Reconstruction period in the 1860s South while depicting blacks as little more than savages. One black given power during the post-Civil War era was described as animalistic, with "sinister bead eyes."[1] The book also portrayed Klansmen as heroic figures who saved the South from Northern Reconstructionist ideology and black domination:

> In the darkest hour of the life of the South, when her wounded people lay helpless amid rags and ashes under the beak and talon of the Vulture, suddenly from the mists of the mountains appeared a

white cloud the size of a man's hand. It grew until its mantle of mystery enfolded the stricken earth and sky. An "Invisible Empire" had risen from the field of Death and challenged the Visible to mortal combat.

How the young South, led by the reincarnated souls of the Clansmen of Old Scotland, went forth under this cover and against overwhelming odds, daring exile, imprisonment, and a felon's death, and saved the life of a people, forms one of the most dramatic chapters in the history of the Aryan race.[2]

Many hard-core racists are sickened by the mere sight of a black walking down the street and thoroughly disgusted at displays of race mixing, particularly mixed marriages. And some even claim that they extracted proof of black inferiority and the dangers of integration from the Bible. Included was James Venable, who was raised in the shadow of Stone Mountain, Georgia, and served as Imperial Wizard of the National Knights of the Klan from 1963 to 1987 before his death in 1993. Venable spoke freely about the supposed differences in blood between whites and blacks. "When you go to mixin' this inferior blood, intermarriage of the black man, you're goin' to destroy both races," he said. "He wants to kill and destroy."[3]

Some Klansmen have refused to believe that any African American boasts the intellectual capacity to be a useful member of society, even after the election of Barack Obama, America's first black president, in 2008. Among them was Imperial Klans of America Imperial Wizard Ron Edwards, who spoke critically not only of Obama, but of how he saw the American mindset in a new age. During the 2008 presidential campaign, Edwards said:

> I don't care that his mother was white, I don't think he has enough brains to do anything good. All he's living off of is the color of his skin to get elected. I don't think America wants a black president. Most of them are too afraid to say that they believe the way I believe. They sit around their dinner table and talk the way I do, but when they get out in public, they have two faces and show the other face. When people are voting in the booth privately, they'll vote Republican even if they're a Democrat.[4]

It has been offered that the German Nazi movement of the 1920s and 1930s borrowed its philosophy from the American Klan, though there has been little proof to back up that claim. However, both have had in common the belief that race has been the driving force between good and evil in the history of humankind. In this era of political correctness, many Klansmen have spoken of their desires for the separation of the races without expressing their perceived black inferiority as the basis of such feelings. But both German Nazis and Klansmen have also shared a conviction that Jews are dangerous as well, due to what they perceive as their control of the media and banking industry and their supposed feelings of moral and intellectual superiority.

Among those who have researched the mindset and philosophies of modern Klansmen and other organized racists such as neo-Nazis is former University of Michigan psychology professor Raphael S. Ezekiel, who went on to study youth violence prevention for the Harvard School of Public Health. Ezekiel wrote:

> The movement today feels itself a defense organization. White rule in America has ended, members feel. A new world they do not like has pushed aside the traditional one they think they remember. In the old world, the only significant people were whites; men struggled as individuals to build a life for their families; good men and dutiful women lived peacefully; somewhere in the background were others. Today, they feel, those others have taken control. The government and high society fawn over the blacks. Blacks are given special privileges and special access to work. Blacks breed recklessly and fill the cities with unloved and illegitimate progeny. Blacks have no feel for honest work; blacks rob or live off welfare; blacks live on drugs. . . . The only good thing that has happened has been the advent of AIDS; "Praise God for AIDS!" the white racists cry out at their rallies.[5]

It has been argued that Klansmen are either too ignorant or stubborn to understand the view that crime in the United States has always been a reflection of socioeconomic place in society and, in fact, ran rampant among all minority groups during their periods in the lower strata of the nation's financial hierarchy. The social changes that have resulted in a huge influx of blacks into the middle and upper classes have thus lowered the rates of criminality, drug addiction, and teenage pregnancy in the black community.

Klan strategy has evolved greatly over the past several decades based on the legal strides finally achieved by blacks through the civil rights movement and a general shift in attitude about race relations in the white community. The legal barriers of segregation and discrimination have been virtually eliminated, giving blacks full rights in the voting process as well as in employment, housing, and education. Though it will likely take several more generations before the economic disparities between whites and blacks are erased, white racists perceive the inferiority of blacks will prevent them from ever achieving equality. Many Klansmen feel the battle for the spoils of the American dream and the inherent inability for whites and blacks to co-exist will eventually lead to a race war in the United States that will once and for all result in the separation of the races. Some even offer dramatically that the race war will prove to be a prelude to Armageddon.

Most Klansmen and other white supremacists believe not only in the biological inferiority of blacks, but also in a modern-day Darwinism once embraced by Hitler and the Nazis. This view asserts that the comparative technological and cultural advancement proves that the Aryan white race is superior to all others and that blacks are the most inferior with various other races falling somewhere in between. They feel the natural order of the human race is no different than that of an animal world in which only the strongest survive. Hard-core racists with a political bent feel a race war will either cleanse America of what they perceive to be the inferior black race or at least provide separation.

One group that has gone so far as to claim that the "purification" of mankind is God's will is Christian Identity, a radical-right, religiously based anti-Semitic and racist organization that traces its roots to the end of World War II and has been connected with the Klan. Ezekiel explained that the Christian Identity view is shared by many white supremacists and white separatists, who scoff at the notion that all men are created equal.

"God, Identity tells us, is white," Ezekiel wrote. "The white race, the Aryans, are His chosen people. The white God has now called his chosen people and drawn them together in America. Here they are to do His bidding, to fulfill His plan for them, which is the domination of the earth."[6]

This philosophy allows politically oriented Klansmen an easy escape for the obvious questions about God's creation of all of mankind and the equality of all of God's children. Those who believe in the Christian Identity theory can still embrace their interpretations of religious teachings as well as the notion of racial inequality. But logical justification for hatred and violence has never proven to be important to hard-core racists such as Klansmen. That's why they've been around, whether in hoods and robes or suits and ties, for 150 years.

NOTES

1. Thomas Dixon, *The Clansman: An Historical Romance of the Ku Klux Klan* (New York: Doubleday, Page & Company, 1905), 216. http://www.archive.org/stream/clansmanhistoric00dixo/clansmanhistoric00dixo_djvu.txt.

2. Thomas Dixon, *The Clansman: An Historical Romance of the Ku Klux Klan*, "To the Reader" (New York: Doubleday, Page & Company, 1905), 216. http://www.archive.org/stream/clansmanhistoric00dixo/clansmanhistoric00dixo_djvu.txt.

3. Patsy Sims, *The Klan* (Lexington, Ky.: The University Press of Kentucky, 1996), 254.

4. David Peisner, "Why White Supremacists Support Barack Obama," *Esquire* online, Oct. 30, 2008. http://www.esquire.com/the-side/feature/racists-support-obama-061308 (accessed February 3, 2009).

5. Raphael S. Ezekiel, *The Racist Mind* (New York: Penguin Books, 1995), xxv–xxvi.

6. Ezekiel, *Racist Mind*, 124.

Who Joins and Why? Mysticism, Politics, and Women of the KKK

Though the political landscape and state of race relations in America have always determined Klan focus and strategy, the attraction of the organization has never been based solely on such considerations. Nor has the KKK ever proved to be a particular lure to those with a political bent.

Indeed, racial bigotry and ethnic and religious intolerance have helped spark many to join the KKK over the past one hundred fifty years. But the huge majority of members have been the downtrodden whites in American society, the frustrated few who couldn't find their professional, social, or economic niche. They looked on the Klan as an organization in which they could feel like someone special. The same held true for those who joined the Nazi movement before it took power in Germany in the 1920s and early 1930s. They, too, were from the lowest classes of that society who had been most affected by the Depression and who sought to blame the Jews for all their ills. They were promised a uniform and camaraderie and a purpose in life shared by and acted on by others. Hitler and his henchmen provided participation in grandiose events with great fanfare, pageantry, and color to spice up the drab and seemingly hopeless lives of Germans, a strategy which eventually led to his taking power in 1933.

The Klan has never gained anything close to such strength in America, though it did count several million among its members in the early 1920s. But throughout the century-and-a-half, it has used the same forms of attraction to motivate the dispirited and angry minority to join. The mystical symbols and titles, hoods and robes, and ritualistic cross-burning ceremonies have seduced millions and given them a sense of power and belonging. And just as the Nazis used that sense of power and belonging to inspire its members to take violent action against Jews, which opened the door for the Holocaust, the Klan used it to incite its members to beat up or even murder blacks and, in more recent years, those deemed undesirables such as Communists, foreigners, and homosexuals.

Southerners angry over the defeat of the Confederacy in the Civil War were the first to be induced by the mysticism of the Klan, though its first membership drive also found success because of bitterness over the political events of the time. Vengeful veterans of the Confederate army, now trained in the use of violence, took out their frustrations on blacks, who were easy targets and whose role in the center of the slavery controversy they blamed for the conflict, as well as Southern Republicans, whom they viewed as traitors. But the Pulaski Six who founded the Klan used a rather light-hearted, yet solemn approach to their early initiations. They created unusual ceremonies in which they rode up as disguised horsemen to men they deemed to be potential members, blindfolded them, and whisked them away to a country plantation that had been destroyed by a December cyclone. A skullcap with donkey's ears sewn on it was placed on the head of a candidate, who was then escorted to a large dressing mirror the Klan dubbed as "the royal altar" and ordered to recite a poem written by Scotsman Robert Burns. The blindfold was then removed to reveal to the candidate that he'd literally been dressed up as an ass, much to the amusement of the Klansmen. The embarrassed man could then accept or deny membership. Most agreed to join with those in the financially depressed rural areas showing a particular interest.

The power of Klan mysticism and fascination of its symbols and rituals were least indicative during its revival, which ran in earnest from 1915 to 1925. The Klan had, at least publicly, eschewed violence toward blacks, Jews, and other minorities, yet membership grew exponentially. It marked the first and only time that the Klan lured in not just the angry and downtrodden, but also typical Americans. The strongest draw was the stated purpose of fighting for Christian morality, which brought with it an underlying notion of inherent superiority to blacks, Jews, and the millions of immigrants streaming toward American shores. The Klan was ostensibly fighting for "family values" more than a half-century before right-wing Americans popularized the term. Although the attraction of donning Klan garb and participating in Klan activities was also a boon to membership, the perceived threat to the fabric of American society proved to be more so. Northwestern University history professor Nancy MacLean wrote:

> To make sense of the Klan [during that era] one must first surrender some comforting illusions. Above all, one has to give up the notion of the essential otherness of the kind of men attracted to it. In the 1920s, at least, Klan members were not the deranged outcasts of popular imagination. A score of historians have now painstakingly researched the membership and activities in Klan chapters in localities across the nation. And they have found that most often the men who donned the order's robes and assembled beneath its flaming crosses were, as one contemporary put it, "if not the best people, at least the next best . . . the good, solid middle-class citizens." Not only did the Klan draw from the broad middle of the nation's class structure, but it most commonly mobilized support through campaigns waged on the prosaic theme of upholding community moral standards.[1]

That middle class was far less likely to be seduced by such so-called inducements as participation in cross burnings and wearing a hood and robe. Those from that socio-economic background were also much less prone to violence as a means to achieve their goals. When reports of Klan violence and immorality were peppered throughout the media in the mid-1920s, the middle class left the organization in droves. It proved to be the last time the KKK wielded any significant power in the United States. From that point forward, the only publicity it garnered was through violence, especially that which resulted in the murder of innocent people and its political enemies. The lynchings, shootings, and bombings that killed hundreds following World War II through the civil rights era were perpetrated

The body of 32-year-old Rubin Stacy hangs from a tree in Fort Lauderdale, Florida, as neighbors visit the site on July 19, 1935. Stacy, who allegedly attacked a white woman, was lynched by a mob of masked men who seized him from the custody of sheriff's deputies. Source: *AP Photo.*

by hard-core Klansmen motivated by anger and hatred, the down-trodden of American society; the vast majority were lured by the sense of belonging provided by the hoods and robes, mystical titles, and cross-burning ceremonies.

The same has held true to a great extent for the women of the Klan, whose numbers grew tremendously during the membership explosion from 1915 to 1925. Women, particularly during that era, were attracted to the Klan for political concerns as well as to maintain a kinship with the men in their lives and for the social opportunities provided them by joining the organization. The huge majority of Klanswomen had boyfriends or husbands who were also members, many of whom had already been initiated. However, this is not to suggest that the estimated 500,000 who made up the Women of the Ku Klux Klan (WKKK), which was founded in 1923 with its national headquarters in Little Rock, Arkansas, weren't driven by the same racist, anti-Semitic, anti-Catholic views as their male brethren. They were also equally motivated by furthering the cause of the same perception of Christian morality held by Klansmen. They were simply utilized differently. University of Kentucky sociology professor Kathleen M. Blee wrote the following about the influence of the WKKK:

> The story of the immense and powerful Klan of the 1920s is incomplete without serious attention to the role of Klanswomen. Not only were women a significant portion of the Klan's membership, but their activities and ideologies differed sufficiently from those of Klansmen that an examination of the women's Klan changes our interpretation of the Klan as a whole. . . . Klanswomen acted in different ways that complemented those of Klansmen, making the Klan's influence both more extensive and more deadly.
> . . . An examination of the role of Klanswomen also reveals the Klan's pervasiveness and subtle influence in the 1920s. Women of the Klan drew on familial and community ties . . . to circulate the Klan's message of racial, religious, and national bigotry. They spread hatred through neighborhoods, family networks, and illusive webs of private relationships.[2]

One might be surprised to note that the Klan officially took a progressive view of women's rights during its heyday, which coincided with the suffrage movement. It viewed women's political role as separate and even subordinate to men, which was certainly not unusual for that era. However, the Klan newspaper, *The Fiery Cross*, came out in favor of the National Women's party campaign to get women elected to Congress as well as the campaign to give women equal representation in the legislative bodies of the Presbyterian Church. Though the Klan hierarchy believed in the purity of women and felt they should remain chaste before marriage, such was also not a radical outlook at the time.

The Klan view was that the role of women was essential to maintaining family values, but that role was not inconsistent with their march toward political equality. In fact, the Klan saw the increased participation of women in government as a means to help clean up corruption. Klan women became part of the temperance movement that led to Prohibition. The Klan took a very practical view of the potential political role of women. The WKKK meant vastly increased membership of both men and women and strengthened the entire agenda, which at the time revolved around its perception of Christian morality.

Blee wrote:

> As the temperance and moral reform movements of the early twentieth century did, the Klan saw women's inherently moral nature as key to campaigns for clean government and control of vice since women would vote for candidates promising to rid the country of liquor, prostitution, and gambling. Without question, the KKK assured its members, bringing white Protestant women into the electoral arena would result in less corrupt politics: "A woman has convictions and ideals, and she is willing to sacrifice party and her own political aspirations for the common good of the country and American ideals."

> One way the Klan handled the apparent lag in gender equality in a Christian nation was to interpret U.S. history to emphasize women's hidden power. . . . Women operated through indirect channels, using their control over the home to exercise power in the outside world. As mothers and wives, women had a role in the world that was at least as influential as man's, even if their formal rights were limited.[3]

Though some in the Klan believed the drive for women to enter the work world was tearing down the fabric of American society and that their proper place was rearing children in the home, its press came out in favor of the economic freedom of women. One publication offered that, "No longer will man say that in the hand of woman rests the necessity of rocking a cradle only. She has within her hand the power to rule the world."[4]

Such a view differed greatly from and seemed inconsistent with the Klan philosophy and outlook on gender that helped make *Birth of a Nation* a huge success and launched the organization's revival. That view was the helplessness and purity of women, who required manhood, specifically Klansmen, to save them from "crazed" blacks who were motivated instinctually to conquer white women.

The Klan downplayed the notion of white superiority and eschewed racial violence to gain millions of members in the early twentieth century. The WKKK adopted the same philosophy and strategy. In pamphlets provided its members, the WKKK espoused quite a tolerant approach to religious freedom and race relations, opting instead to emphasize its dedication to the United States and its Constitution, a document that had been figuratively torn to shreds by the Klan in previous years. Though the WKKK believed in black inferiority, it was ostensibly an organization that would protect the rights for all Americans.

One pamphlet read:

> The Women of the Ku Klux Klan . . . STANDS ABSO-LUTELY FOR THE PROTECTION OF PURE AMERICAN WOMANHOOD.
>
> It is essentially Militantly Patriotic in principle and lofty in its Ideals, having no thought of self or gain, but an everlasting determination to keep for Americans and those within the territorial boundaries of the UNITED STATES OF AMERICA the lofty principles of self-government, constitutional rights, and the pursuit of happiness as guaranteed by the constitution of the UNITED STATES.
>
> . . . It is composed only of Protestant women; therefore, only Protestant women can attain membership.
>
> It is composed only of Native Born American Women, therefore no women of foreign birth is eligible to citizenship in the Invisible Empire.
>
> These restrictions are not intended to cast aspersions upon the Patriotism and other great and noble qualities of women of other faiths and other nationalities. We acknowledge the fact that a great majority of them are just as Patriotic and have just as many good qualities as we, but our Constitutional limits are set as above outlined, and we can not deviate therefrom.
>
> One of the IDEALS and teachings of the WOMEN OF THE KU KLUX KLAN is the eternal SUPREMACY of the WHITE race; therefore, only white women can become members.
>
> IT BELIEVES THAT THE NEGRO SHOULD BE PRO-TECTED in every way possible and will as readily fight for their

Constitutional rights or, for that matter, those for any other persons, as for its own."[5]

The collapse of the Klan in the late 1920s also spelled the end of extensive female involvement in the organization. But based on the violent and even murderous actions undertaken during the civil rights movement and beyond, many believed it to be absurd that Klansmen or Klanswomen would honestly support or fight for the Constitutional rights of a black race they have always considered inferior.

A member of the Ladies' Auxiliary of the United Klans of America, Inc., holds her young daughter, also robed in a Klan suit, at a Ku Klux Klan rally in Atlanta, Georgia, 1965. Although extensive female Klan membership ended by the late 1920s, some women were still in the Klan decades later. Source: *AP Photo.*

NOTES

1. Nancy McLean, *Behind the Mask of Chivalry: The Making of the Second Ku Klux Klan* (New York: Oxford University Press, 1994), xii.
2. Kathleen M. Blee, *Women of the Klan*, (Los Angeles: University of California Press, 1991), 2–3.
3. Ibid., 50.
4. Lois Carlson, "The Sanctity of the Home," *The Kourier Magazine*, June 1929, 46–47.
5. Women of the Ku Klux Klan, *Women of America! The Past! The Present! The Future! Outline of Principles and Teachings*, The Online Books Page: Online Books of Women of the Ku Klux Klan. http://onlinebooks.library.upenn.edu/webbin/book/lookupname?key=Women%20of%20the%20Ku%20Klux%20Klan (accessed February 5, 2009).

Conclusion

From Reconstruction to the civil rights movement and beyond, Klansmen have defended violence and even murder by claiming such actions were done in the name of Americanism. Klan leaders have spewed forth their beliefs from rural clearings, halls of justice, and the sites of bloody Civil War battles that the United States was created as a white, Protestant nation, that blacks are genetically inferior, that Jews are the children of the devil, and that immigrants disgrace the American shores on which they land.

Despite the proclamations of the Declaration of Independence—that all men are created equal and are endowed by their creator with the right to life, liberty, and pursuit of happiness—that has certainly not always held true in the nation's history. For nearly two centuries, blacks were enslaved and deemed as just three-fifths of a person. Laws have also prevented Jews and women from taking their rightful places in society. But for the most part, America has at least strived to live out its creed. Civil rights laws enacted in the 1960s wiped out the last vestiges of legalized racism.

Though the 1990s and the new millennium brought forth far greater militancy from the radical right, the target for violence has shifted from individual blacks or Jews to the overthrow of the U.S. government. But throughout American history, only the Klan has consistently heaped terror on its citizens.

The motivation of Klansmen has remained the same since six former Confederate officers from Pulaski, Tennessee, met in the law office of Calvin Jones and created what soon developed into a terrorist organization. From the Reconstruction era forward, they have fought violently against integration, driven by the perception that black equality would translate into the deterioration of American society.

It has been generally accepted in the United States that racist fears are based on hatred and ignorance. After all, if they truly believed in the sanctity and righteousness of the Declaration of Independence, the argument goes, they wouldn't have taken such violent actions to prevent blacks from securing their equal rights. They also wouldn't foster such hatred and mistrust of Jews, Catholics, and immigrants. It is possible that in a country of 300 million people, there will always be a fringe element bent on creating chaos. We as a society have generally applauded groups such as Klanwatch that have reined in the Klan and other radical, violent right-wing organizations.

What must be discussed, then, is how the Klan has affected America as a whole or, more specifically, how Americans have reacted to the Klan. And that has changed from era to era based on Klan philosophies, the social and economic climate of the country, and the mindset of its people.

Most obvious is the fact that Americans in general have reviled Klan violence. They have been least accepting of the Klan during its most violent periods, particularly in the late 1950s and early 1960s. Certainly Americans by that time had grown more tolerant of those the Klan railed against, such as blacks and Jews. However, it can be argued successfully that the revelation of similar Klan violence in the 1920s produced a mass exodus from its membership rolls.

The Klan has been most accepted during periods in which it espoused its perception of Christian morality and presented (disguised?) itself as more of a social club than a terrorist organization. Certainly, anti-immigration and the notion of black inferiority had been widely embraced during the great Klan expansion from 1915 to 1925, but membership soared not because of racist, anti-Semitic sentiment or prejudice against foreigners. It grew to more than 4 million due to its championing of civic pride and responsibility, as well as a sense of family and belonging. If the hatred of others or even maintaining the segregationist policies of that era had been the primary promotions of the Klan, it may be that few would have joined.

America was founded on the principle of freedom and justice for all, and though those rights weren't enjoyed by African Americans, particularly in the South, a general belief in that righteousness of that philosophy has always played a large role in the reaction of the American public to Klan violence. During the civil rights movement, even some Americans who did not support civil rights were disgusted by such violent excesses as the bombing of a Birmingham church that snuffed out the lives of four black children.

The most significant changes in American race relations over the past forty years have occurred in the South. Where once Klansmen roamed free to bomb homes and churches, lynch blacks, and murder their political enemies with nary the slightest fear that an all-white jury would convict them, some are now spending the rest of their lives in jail or have died there. Others have repented and apologized for their actions.

Among the most publicized cases was that of former Klansman Elwin Wilson, who in 1961 had beaten a Freedom Rider named John Lewis when the latter attempted to help integrate a bus terminal in Rock Hill, South Carolina. Early in 2009, Wilson came to Washington, D.C., to visit with and apologize to Lewis, who was now a United States congressman. Instead of reaching his hand out with a clenched fist, as he had done forty-eight years earlier, Wilson extended his hand to shake that of Lewis in front of a national television audience watching on *Good Morning America*. The two later embraced as Lewis explained that he had already forgiven Wilson. Other stories of repentant Klansmen have dotted the media landscape in recent years.

The Klan has been relegated to an afterthought in our society. It is considered by most people as no more than a band of hooded racists whose members once terrorized blacks and other perceived political enemies. It has even taken a back seat in the fears of Americans to more militant groups bent on the violent overthrow of the government. Watchdog organizations that have kept a keen eye on all radical and potentially violent right-wing extremist groups have served to allay the fears of a Klan revival.

It has been said that anyone who believes the Klan will remain a nonentity is being far too hopeful or far too ignorant. After all, the same was claimed in the late 1800s, during World War II, and in the early 1970s. And the Klan proved after each one of those eras that it was indeed not ready for the grave. But integration and the acceptance of other races and cultures in America do give legitimization to the belief that the Klan could never achieve the influence it gained in previous generations. This is not the segregated America of the 1920s. This is the America that elected a black president in 2008, a happening that would have been considered unthinkable even a quarter-century earlier.

Klansmen have been fighting a losing battle since they first donned a hood and robe. They were trying to maintain or create inequality in a nation founded, at least in theory, on the belief that all men and women are created equal.

Biographical Sketches

The Enigma: Nathan Bedford Forrest

One who drives around Kentucky Lake and near tiny Eva, Tennessee, might be taken aback by the name of one particular recreational area. It's called Nathan Bedford Forrest State Park. That same traveler would be equally surprised as he heads further south to note the name of an educational facility in Jacksonville, Florida: Nathan Bedford Forrest High School.

That two such entities bear the name of an early Ku Klux Klan leader could shock Americans, particularly in an era of sensitivity and political correctness. But therein lies the incongruity surrounding Forrest's life, including his heroism during the Civil War and his role in the KKK. Many insist that Forrest was indeed a military hero and that his involvement with the Klan ended when its members began using violent tactics to intimidate and even murder blacks and those who sought to educate the freed slaves.

The controversy regarding Forrest continues to rage. In fact, the Duval County School Board, which governs Nathan Bedford Forrest High, met in November 2008 to decide whether to change the name of the school, which had been chosen in the 1950s by a group that called itself the Daughters of the Confederacy in a response to the landmark Supreme Court ruling in *Brown v. Board of Education* that cleared the way for the integration of American public schools. The Duval County board voted five to two to keep the name. The five who voted in favor were white. The two who voted to change the name of the school were black.

Forrest was the first of twelve children born into a poor family in Chapel Hill, Tennessee. His mother, Miriam, stayed home with the kids while his father, William, a blacksmith, tried to make ends meet. But when William died, his eldest child was forced to become head of the household at age seventeen.

In 1841, the teenager joined his uncle's business in Hermando, Mississippi. But soon thereafter his uncle was killed during an argument with several brothers of the Matlock family. Forrest joined the fray and killed two of the Matlocks with a pistol and wounded two others by hurling knives at them. Strangely, one of the Matlocks who survived served under Forrest during the Civil War.

Forrest wasn't poor for long. After settling in Memphis in 1852, he did well enough in the slave trading business to purchase two plantations and amass a fortune estimated at $1.5 million. But the potential abolishment of slavery motivated Forrest to join the Confederate army as a mere private on June 14, 1861. And despite a distinct lack of military training, Forrest emerged as one of the most prominent and respected cavalry leaders of the war. He proved impressive enough from the beginning of the conflict to motivate Confederate leaders to allow him to form his own mounted battalion, though it was done at his own expense. By October 1861, Forrest had worked his way up to lieutenant colonel. By the end of the Civil War, he served as a brigadier general. In between, he held more than a dozen posts and had fought with armies in Tennessee, Mississippi, Louisiana, Alabama, and Georgia.

Early in the war, Forrest made a name for himself by saving his besieged troops after a failed Confederate breakout. He directed his rear guard around enemy lines in retreats from Nashville and Shiloh. Following the latter retreat, Forrest was wounded, but he recovered to be promoted to brigadier general, during which time he raised a brigade with which he captured Murfreesboro, including its garrison and supplies.

Forrest spearheaded another raid in late 1862 and early 1863 in West Tennessee that resulted in the suspension of Union General Ulysses S. Grant's campaign in central Mississippi. Several months later, he helped capture a Union raiding column, but soon thereafter he was shot again, this time by a disenchanted subordinate named Andrew W. Gould. Forrest retaliated by mortally wounding Gould

Nathan Bedford Forrest

with a penknife. After recovering from his gunshot wound, Forrest led an attack that resulted in the capturing of Fort Pillow and a Confederate victory at Brice's Crossroads. But his pathetically small force could do little against the Union onslaught in Alabama and Georgia at the end of the war.

One particular controversy followed Forrest into peacetime. And that was slaughter of an entire garrison of black Union soldiers at Fort Pillow, for which President Andrew Johnson pardoned him after the war. ". . . It was more than one survivor of that battle could stomach," offered Wyn Craig Wade in his book, *The Fiery Cross: The Ku Klux Klan in America.* "He wrote to Senator Benjamin Wade deploring the fact that such 'a foul fiend in human shape' as Forrest, well known for his 'butchery and barbarity' had received such a swift, unconditional pardon instead of 'the punishment which his atrocious crimes so richly deserve.'"[1]

A *New York Times* account of the Fort Pillow incident published as part of his obituary in 1877 blamed Forrest for the massacre:

> It is in connection with one of the most atrocious and cold-blooded massacres that ever disgraced civilized warfare this his name will forever be inseparably associated. "Fort Pillow Forrest" was the title which the deed conferred on him, and by this he will be remembered by the present generation, and by it he will pass into history. The massacre occurred on the 12th of April, 1864. Fort Pillow is 65 miles above Memphis, and its capture was effected during Forrest's celebrated raid through Tennessee, a State which was at the time practically in possession of the Union forces . . .
>
> Late in March (Forrest) passed into that State, and the route of his advance was marked by outrages and brutalities of the most cold-blooded character. He captured most of the small garrisons on his line of march, in each case summoning the defenders to surrender under a threat that if he had to storm the works he would give no quarter. On the 12th of April he appeared before Fort Pillow. The fort was garrisoned by 500 troops, about half of them colored. Forrest's force numbered about 5,000 or 6,000. His first attack was a complete surprise, and the commanding officer was killed in the engagement. Still the defenders fought so gallantly that at 2 o-clock the enemy had gained no material advantage. Forrest then sent in a

flag of truce, demanding unconditional surrender. After a short consultation, Major Bradford, on whom the command had devolved, sent word refusing to surrender. Instantly, the bugles sounded the assault. The enemy were now within 100 yards of the fort, and at the sound they rushed to the works, shouting. The garrison was seized with a panic: the men threw down their arms and sought safety in flight toward the river, in the neighboring ravine, behind logs, bushes, trees, and in fact everywhere where there was a chance for concealment. It was in vain. The captured fort and its vicinity became a human shambles. Without discrimination of age or sex, men, women, and children, the sick and wounded in the hospitals, were butchered without mercy. The bloody work went on until night put a temporary stop to it; but it was renewed at early dawn, when the inhuman captors searched the vicinity of the fort, dragging out wounded fugitives and killing them where they lay. The whole history of the affair was brought out by a Congressional inquiry, and the testimony presents a long series of sickening, cold-blooded atrocities.

Forrest reported his own loss at 20 killed and 60 wounded; and states that he buried 228 Federals on the evening of the assault. Yet in the face of this, he claimed that the Fort Pillow capture was "a bloody victory, only made a massacre by dastardly Yankee reporters." The news of the massacre aroused the whole country to a paroxysm of horror and fury.

. . . Since the war, Forrest has lived in Memphis, and his principal occupation seems to have been to try and explain away the Fort Pillow affair. He wrote several letters about it, which were published, and always had something to say about it any public speech he delivered. He seemed as if he were trying always to rub away the blood stains which marked him.[2]

The defeat of the Confederacy and abolishment of slavery proved to be the end of Forrest's elite financial status. He emerged from the war as little more than a beggar, which humiliated what was a proud man. His wealth was wiped out by the war, but he recovered to become president of the Selma, Marion & Memphis Railroad. And in 1867, Captain John W. Morton, who had served under Forrest during the war, decided his former commander would be an ideal choice to take over as Klan Grand Wizard for the Realm of Tennessee. Not only was Forrest a respected military leader, but his name was also well-known throughout the South, a fact that Morton surmised would result in the growth of the Klan outside the area of Tennessee in which it was founded. Moreover, Morton believed that Forrest's standing as a railroad entrepreneur would add a touch of high society to an organization rapidly becoming known as attractive merely to the disenfranchised.

Forrest accepted the position and set out to make the Invisible Empire quite visible. He understood that riding and terrorizing in the dead of night was no way to positively publicize the Klan, so he organized parades and openly advertised den meetings and initiation ceremonies in newspapers throughout, around, and beyond middle and western Tennessee. Among them was the following published in the *Tuscaloosa* (Alabama) *Independent Monitor*:

Shrouded Brotherhood! Murdered heroes!

Fling the bloody dirt that covers you to the four winds! Erect thy Goddess on the banks of the Avernus. Mark well your foes! Strike with the red-hot spear! Prepare Charon for his task!

Enemies reform! The skies shall be blackened! A single Star shall look down upon horrible deeds! The night owl shall hoot a requiem o'er Ghostly Corpses!

Beware! Beware! Beware!

The Great Cyclops is angry! Hobgoblins report! Shears and lash!

Tar and feathers! Hell and Fury!

Revenge! Revenge! Revenge!

Bad men! White, black, yellow, repent!

The hour is at hand! Be ye ready! Life is short!

. . . Ghosts! Ghosts! Ghosts!

Drink thy tea made of distilled hell, stirred with the lightning of heaven, and sweetened with the gall of thine enemies!

All will be well![3]

The night that warning appeared in the paper, three black men were dragged from their beds, escorted a mile to the outskirts of

Tuscaloosa and severely beaten. It was that growing form of intimidation and violence that alarmed Forrest. In August 1867, the state
legislature gave blacks the right to vote, a process that drew surpris-
ingly little interference from the Klan, greatly because Forrest
worked to keep the members in line. He even warned General
George H. Thomas, who served as the U.S. military commander
of the district, that the animosity between the Irish and black population of the area might result in the inability of the latter to
exercise their right to vote. Forrest and the Klan did have an ulte-
rior motive in their hope that blacks, who had been told by conservatives that their former masters had their best interests at
heart, would vote Democratic. But when blacks heeded the Union
League call and voted for Republicans, who had spearheaded the
anti-slavery campaign, white anger at both blacks and anyone
helping them become acclimated to freedom boiled over with the
Klan leading the attacks. In an interview granted to the *Cincinnati
Commercial* in 1868, Forrest offered that the Klan was not as much
motivated by racism as it was by the actions of Union League
members. His words echoed widely believed white sentiment that
blacks were incapable of independently judging the merits of various candidates and parties and were persuaded by others to vote
Republican.

Meanwhile, Forrest continued to recruit new members. By the
time he was named Grand Wizard, the Klan had leaked into Mississippi and Alabama simply because of those states' proximity to Tennessee. But between January and May of 1868, he scoured the
South to not only add membership, but also to seek out leaders. He
appointed former Confederate General John B. Gordon as Georgia's
first Grand Dragon. And Forrest's visits to North Carolina and
South Carolina provided active Klan membership in those states.
Soon the Klan spread like wildfire into Kentucky, West Virginia,
and even Maryland and Missouri.

The number of Klansman was growing, but much to Forrest's
dismay, so were incidents of violence, particularly in Tennessee. No
longer could he, nor even those in power beneath him, control the
Ghouls. Forrest's January 1869 edict that for all intents and purposes called for the disbandment of the Klan simply served to end
his relationship with the organization.

The Marion & Memphis Railroad faltered in the early 1870s, which sent Forrest reeling financially again. He spent his later years running a prison farm along the Mississippi River before his death in October 1877. But according to the announcement of his passing in the *New York Times*, his attitude toward blacks had changed in his final years:

> Of late years, his views had undergone a considerable change. The guerrilla chieftain had softened down into the retired veteran, anxious, apparently, only for peace with everybody. He was in favor of promoting good feeling between the two sections, and by the terms of his address to his old comrades in arms, asking them to join in decorating the graves of the dead Union soldiers. His last notable public appearance was on the Fourth of July in Memphis, when he appeared before the colored people at their celebration, was publicly presented with a bouquet by them as a mark of peace and reconciliation, and made a friendly speech in reply. In this he once more took occasion to defend himself and his war record, and to declare that he was a hearty friend of the colored race. Gen. Forrest would be remembered only as a daring and successful guerrilla cavalry leader, were it not for the one great and indelible stain upon his name. It was evident that he felt this, as his constantly repeated defenses of himself show. His daring and recklessness gave him more eclat at one period than his military services were really entitled to. Gen. Wheeler's raid around the rear of Sherman's army was the work of the daring man and the scientific soldier; Gen. Forrest's sudden dash through Memphis, with no more result than the killing of a few men on either side, was the recklessness of the mere guerrilla chief—which Forrest essentially was.[4]

Forrest's grandson and great-grandson both followed in his footsteps, the latter in a more heroic manner. Grandson and namesake Nathan Bedford Forrest spent part of the 1920s as the Grand Dragon of Georgia. Nathan Bedford Forrest III earned the rank of brigadier general in the United States Air Force and was killed in 1943 during a bombing raid over Germany. He was the first U.S. general killed during the war.

NOTES

1. Wyn Craig Wade, *The Fiery Cross: The Ku Klux Klan in America* (New York: Simon and Schuster, 1987), 16–17.
2. "Death of Gen. Forrest," *New York Times*, Oct. 30, 1877. http://www.nytimes. com/learning/general/onthisday/bday/0713.html (accessed January 27, 2009).
3. Walter L. Fleming, "Prescript of the Ku Klux Klan," *Publications of the Southern History Association*, September 1903, 327.
4. "Death of Gen. Forrest," *New York Times*, Oct. 30, 1877. http://www.nytimes. com/learning/general/onthisday/bday/0713.html (accessed January 27, 2009).

The Revivalist: William Joseph Simmons

Of all the radical, right-wing, racist zealots inhabiting the South in the early twentieth century, none might have seemed less likely to usher in the only highly influential Klan era in America than an alcoholic preacher named William Joseph Simmons.

But then, Simmons himself might not have been surprised. His opinion of himself was noted to be far loftier than that of others, which led the famed attorney of that era, Clarence Darrow, to offer that, "the number of people on the borderline of insanity in a big country is simply appalling, and those seem especially addicted to believing themselves saviors and prophets."[1]

Darrow was speaking in general terms and not specifically about Simmons, but his words certainly fit the circumstances. No more telling story of Simmons' instability and loneliness was told than that of one drunken summer night at his home as he stared out the window. Simmons spoke about seeing a vision of ghost riders in the sky, racing through the clouds and heavens while the moon's surface was transformed into a relief map of the United States. Simmons dropped to his knees and begged God for an explanation. But though none was forthcoming, Simmons asserted that vision provided him with a divine heralding of his true calling.

From the moment he was born to the wife of a nondescript physician in Harpersville, Alabama, to the time he was selected Imperial Wizard of the reincarnated Klan, Simmons struggled to find his way in life. He claimed to have studied medicine at Johns Hopkins University, though efforts to find the truth have never substantiated it. He fought briefly in the Spanish-American War in the late nineteenth century before attending a revival meeting that converted him into a born-again Christian. He studied theology at Southern University, after which he received his license as a Methodist minister. Simmons began preaching around the South for very little pay and rarely earned more than $300 in a year. That meager income forced him to give public speeches about various moral and topical issues. It was in speaking in front of audiences, particularly in nonreligious environments, in which he found his greatest success.

Considered by many a dreamer who overrated his own talents and potential, Simmons believed he was on the verge of a huge promotion when he attended the 1912 Methodist Bishop's Conference. He expected to land in a church housed in a major city such as Mobile or Montgomery, but was about to receive the shock of his life. Rather than receiving praise, he instead was chastised before the committee, charged with inefficiency, and suspended for one year. He collapsed emotionally, falling into a deep depression, during which time he stayed in a Birmingham boarding house run by relatives.

Simmons managed to stay afloat financially, but couldn't find his niche until he jumped at the opportunity to toil as the Atlanta-area promoter for the Woodmen of the World. During the early part of the 1900s, dozens of fraternal organizations had sprouted up, including the Woodmen, Moose, and Redmen. Simmons threw himself into his work and re-established himself as a social butterfly after years of self-imposed exile. Already a member of two different churches, he also joined several other lodges, including the Masons, Knights of Pythias, and Odd Fellows.

Promoted to district manager for the Woodmen in 1914, Simmons wore his pride on his sleeve—and he wore his lodge pins everywhere. At 6-foot 2-inches tall with bright red hair and a gold-framed pince-nez hanging from a chain clipped to his right earlobe, he was a rather curious sight walking the streets of Atlanta. He soon began referring to himself as Colonel Simmons in reference to his honorary rank with the Woodmen. But his close associates spoke of him and his social attributes with the "half-condemning, half-affectionate, sometimes profane phrases reserved for the amiably fraudulent who managed to be equally at home leading prayer, preaching, taking a dram, or making a fourth at poker."[2]

Simmons might have been lucky in poker, but he was the victim of terrible luck one day in 1915. He was standing on an Atlanta street corner when a touring car screeched out of control and hit him in the back. He was fortunate to have not been killed, but his injuries forced him to be confined to a hospital bed for the next three months. He took full advantage of his time to think. He harkened back to the night that he saw visions of ghost riders in the sky, then began to ponder about *The Clansman*, a book written by Tom Dixon a decade earlier that had recently been made into the epic motion picture, *Birth of a Nation*. He considered the immense popularity of the film and began fermenting in his mind the notion of reviving the Ku Klux Klan.

Simmons soon became obsessed with the idea. He sketched figures of Klansmen both on horseback and on foot from his hospital bed. He ordered a copy of the Klan Prescript that had been created during the Reconstruction period in 1867 and set out to broaden the organization through an expanded terminology and number of rituals and leaders. He fervently worked on placing a "*KL*" in front of every new office title and function, such as the *Kloran* for the Klan constitution. Simmons even created catchy abbreviated passwords such as *AYAK* for "Are You a Klansman?" and *AKIA* for "A Klansman I Am." He used his experience with the Woodmen and knowledge gained as a member of many fraternal orders to formulate a new Klan prospectus. On its completion, he crowed, "It is altogether original, weird, mystical, and of a high class. . . . It unfolds a spiritual philosophy that has to do with the very fundamentals of life and living, here and hereafter."[3]

Soon Simmons and his group of followers were on Stone Mountain reviving the Klan. Though he made certain many of the same Klan rituals from a half-century before were followed, he used a new one that would mesmerize Klansmen and terrorize their many enemies for generations to come. And that was the burning cross. Simmons stole the idea from the fertile imagination of Dixon's book *The Clansman* in which burning crosses were used to send signal fires from one clan to another.

There was one problem, however. Now that Simmons had brought the Klan back to life, he didn't know what the organization and its members should do. The new Klan was in danger of settling in as just another fraternal group, albeit with a name that harkened back to an earlier time. It took charter member Jonathan Frost to give it direction. The racist editor of an Atlanta magazine spearheaded a drive that advanced a philosophy of white supremacy and Christian morality the KKK embraced for generations. Klan publications began spewing forth offerings about the distinctions between races and religions having been decreed by God.

While the Klan promoted the notion of such distinctions between races, Simmons struggled to find distinctions between his organization and the hundreds of others that had sprung forth in the early twentieth century. He and the Klan backed President Woodrow Wilson's policies during World War I and even paraded in the streets of Montgomery, Alabama, in an effort to convince folks to purchase war bonds—not exactly a controversial or unusual pursuit at the time. It wasn't until Simmons reluctantly paid Clarke and Tyler of the Southern Publicity Association to promote the Klan that it hit its stride.

Many believe the Imperial Wizard was simply in over his head once the Klan boom of the early 1920s began in earnest. He earned $170,000 in commissions from membership dues and income from the purchase of various Klan paraphernalia, but wasn't particularly active. Following the *New York World* exposé, however, he did welcome a House investigation into Klan activities that exonerated the organization. In fact, he sent telegrams to every House member asking for a "yes" vote on the bill proposing such an investigation. Simmons understood only through such an official inquiry could the Klan gain respectability and flourish.

That it did to the tune of an estimated 4 million members by 1923. But by that time, Simmons had been conned out of his Wizardship (see Hiram Wesley Evans bio) and kicked "upstairs" to the figurehead position of Emperor. Simmons fought vainly to regain his post but was forced to settle for that greatly honorary position at a salary of $1,000 a month. He attempted to wield power, but to no avail.

The beginning of the end of Simmons' relationship with the Klan occurred after he publicly denounced new Imperial Wizard

Hiram Wesley Evans, who in turn sued him for libel. Soon there-after, a minor official at the Imperial Palace murdered Simmons' at-torney, William S. Coburn. The incident, with which Evans claimed to be uninvolved, frightened Simmons. And on February 12, 1924, he agreed to accept a $145,000 cash settlement to leave the Klan permanently.

Simmons received only $90,000 of that money, most of which he spent creating a rival to the Klan that he dubbed the Knights of the Flaming Sword. He believed the Klan under Evans lost what he perceived to be its religious idealism, which he attempted to instill in his new organization. But the Knights of the Flaming Sword barely got off the ground, greatly because on February 21, 1925, he lost control of his car and slammed into an embankment, killing his passenger instantly. Simmons wound up with four broken ribs and a punctured lung. The slow and painful recovery period precluded any possibility of Simmons promoting his new Knights. The thoroughly defeated former Wizard remained in Atlanta for a few years, then returned to his native Alabama, where he drank heavily and drifted from one rundown hotel to the next until his death on May 18, 1945.

Ironically, Simmons died just eleven days after the surrender of Nazi Germany, which based its racial philosophies along the same lines as did the Klan that Simmons resurrected thirty years earlier.

NOTES

1. Clarence Darrow, *The Story of My Life* (New York: Scribners, 1960), 279.
2. Ralph McGill, *The South and the Southerner* (Boston: Little, Brown, 1963), 131.
3. Wyn Craig Wade, *The Fiery Cross: The Ku Klux Klan in America* (New York: Simon and Schuster, 1987), 143.

The Dentist: Hiram Wesley Evans

If anyone personified the worldview of the Klan leadership during the 1920s, it was Hiram Wesley Evans. This politically oriented Texas dentist saw religious and racial groups in terms of their impact on American society.

No more glaring statements of Evans' outlook and prejudices were made than the ones he expressed as the Klan's second Imperial Wizard in a pamphlet in 1924. "The Negro is not the menace to Americanism in the same sense that the Jew or the Roman Catholic is a menace," he wrote. "He is not actually hostile to it. He is simply racially incapable of understanding, sharing, or contributing to Americanism."[1]

Like so many Klan leaders throughout history, Evans was born in the Deep South, but his family moved from Alabama to Texas during his childhood. He studied dentistry at Vanderbilt University, but whether he ever received his degree remains unclear. In fact, it has been offered that Evans obtained his license from a correspondence school and has even been suggested that he was actually a veterinary dentist. Whatever the case, his Dallas practice thrived.

Swept up in the Klan boom that followed the release of the movie *Birth of a Nation*, Evans joined the organization in 1920 and quickly established himself as the head of the Dallas Klavern and an electrifying speaker. He continued to rise in the Klan hierarchy, earning a term as Great Titan of Province #2 in Texas before Klan promoters Edward Young Clarke and Elizabeth Tyler convinced Imperial Wizard William Simmons to promote Evans to Imperial Kligrapp—national secretary. The move raised Evans' annual salary to a then-lofty $7,500, plus a cut from all fees pouring in from the thirteen Klan charter states. In that capacity, he traveled extensively and developed relationships with state and local Klan officials.

Among those with whom he came into contact was Indiana Klansman David Curtis Stephenson, whose political knowledge and outlook impressed Evans far more than those of Simmons, whom he considered politically disinterested, naïve, and ineffective. Despite the fact that Simmons had only recently promoted Evans to a national office, Evans and Stephenson plotted to oust Simmons from the position of Imperial Wizard and share that power between them. The chicanery was about to begin.

The first step was sending the unwitting Simmons on vacation, which allowed the equally unwitting Clarke to take over the reins temporarily. Meanwhile, Evans schemed with Simmons away and the 1922 Klonvocation (national convention) on the horizon. The event, slated to be a celebration of the reborn Klan's seventh anniversary, was scheduled for the week of Thanksgiving and was to be held in an auditorium on the site of Civil War battlefields. With Klansmen streaming in to Atlanta from throughout the country, Stephenson arranged to convince the delegates to vote Evans in as Imperial Wizard.

Simmons caught wind of the plot and gave a stirring speech to the delegates on the first day, leading them in a rendition of "Onward Christian Soldiers" with tears welling up in his eyes. That night, Stephenson and newly appointed Klan Department of Investigation head Fred Savage contacted every delegate with the news that the election for Imperial Wizard would take place the following day and added that, as both Imperial Wizard and Emperor, Simmons was overworked. Klan Emperor was merely an honorary and spiritual title and required little work, but Stephenson and Savage nevertheless lied to the delegates, telling them that Simmons yearned for an assistant to assume the role of Imperial Wizard and that Evans would be the ideal choice.

Convinced they had taken control of the delegates, they began working on Simmons, whom they awoke at four in the morning with the story that the excitement of the Klonvocation left them unable to sleep. They asked the dazed Wizard about his plans for the election, to which Simmons responded that he assumed the delegates would vote unanimously to keep him in that position. That's when Stephenson and Savage told him a bedtime fairy tale.

"Well, Colonel," Savage began, "we both dropped around to tell you that, whatever happens on the convention floor tomorrow, there will be armed men stationed around the floor to protect your honor." Stephenson went on to say to the stunned Klan leader that a number of insurgents planned on denouncing him, but that "the first man who insults your name will be killed by a sharpshooter right on the spot as he speaks. There will be enough of us with firearms to take care of the whole convention, if necessary." They went on to say that if Simmons wished to avert bloodshed, he could simply recommend Evans for the office of Imperial Wizard and that they would in turn give the Emperor position significant power.[2]

The deed was done. Simmons, who claimed to have nearly collapsed at the notion of a shootout at the Klonvocation, announced that he would be willing to have Evans chosen by the delegates as the new Imperial Wizard, which they did by acclamation. Evans certainly wasted no time embracing his new position; Simmons found him sitting in his old desk at the Imperial Palace several days later. Evans promised Simmons a throne room from which he could serve as Emperor, but it never materialized. In fact, Evans, who set out to turn the Klan into a political power in America, withdrew all his promises to Simmons regarding real authority as Emperor, leaving the ousted Wizard with little more than an honorary title.

The battle was not over. Simmons embarked on a tour in 1923 in an attempt to inform fellow Klansmen of the deception that caused him to lose his position, but Evans showed up at each stop with an injunction that barred the frustrated former Imperial Wizard from speaking. Finally fed up, Simmons obtained a court injunction that handed him temporary control of the Klan and its treasury and even barred Evans from the Palace. Six days later, Evans won a decision in court that allowed him back in the Palace, but also placed the Klan in the hands of a three-man commission. Now neither Simmons nor Evans wielded the power both desperately wanted. The commission hoped to settle matters by allowing a fifteen-member Kloncilium to determine the rightful Wizard. That group consisted of five members chosen by both Evans and Simmons, as well as five Klansmen-at-large, all of whom were loyal to the former. In fact, Stephenson chaired the Kloncilium, which, needless to say, resulted in Evans being chosen as Imperial Wizard.

The decision, however, didn't provide Evans complete power. Simmons still owned the copyright to Klan rituals, titles, regalia, and charter. But the $145,000 cash settlement to Simmons in 1924 finally ended the legal and verbal squabbles and allowed Evans to freely direct the organization. He certainly had some definite ideas, including the near-elimination of the religious fervor that had permeated the promotion of the Klan and motivated hundreds of thousands to join. Instead, Evans played up such angles as superpatriotism, far right-wing political activism, and anti-immigration. He considered the huge influx of immigrants a threat to the purity of American culture. Because the Klan ideals of anti-Catholic, anti-Semitic, and white supremacist sentiment had already been cemented and, while encouraged by Evans, the immigrant threat was not prioritized by the new Klan leader in the mid-1920s.

Rather, he advocated the notion of "klannishness" as the ultimate member virtue. He forwarded the practice of helping fellow Klansmen, as well as other like-minded white Protestants, both personally and professionally. Businesses run by Klansmen began advertising in Klan publications while Evans encouraged members to boycott companies that expressed anti-Klan sentiment. When Fuller Brush Company president Alfred Fuller condemned the Klansmen as fools and radicals, members boycotted his products until he was forced to withdraw his criticism a month later. As Klan membership was reaching its peak, Evans wielded tremendous power not only within the organization, but also throughout America, particularly in the South, Southwest, Northwest, and Midwest.

Evans, however, wasn't satisfied. He convoked his Grand Dragons in July 1923 in Asheville, North Carolina, and expressed to them his desire to double membership, which would raise the count to a whopping 10 million. He stressed that it meant greater civic involvement in the local Klan communities. He spoke about the importance of visibility, whether that was achieved through an increased number of publications or more public rallies and events. Evans also stated his belief that Klansmen should become more active politically at the local and state levels.

Like Simmons, Evans realized that no American organization could thrive using violence mindlessly or even as a means to an end. Unlike Simmons, he didn't deny that Klan violence existed. Evans also understood that one of the nation's foundations was its justice system. He urged his Grand Dragons to ensure that lawbreakers, even those donning Klan hoods and robes, would pay for their crimes. And though he never railed against the immorality of violence, he did consider it, to borrow a term from a later generation, politically incorrect.

Stopping Klan violence was easier said than done. Though the Klan had to some degree reached the mainstream of American society, it remained most attractive to hardened racists for whom violence was a way of life. Evans knew that there was no greater obstacle to his plan to add millions to the Klan membership rolls than incidents of violence that would invariably be pounced on by the print media. One example occurred in tiny Mer Rouge, Louisiana, where Klansmen abducted two white men who vociferously disagreed with their views, beat them unmercifully, ran over them repeatedly with heavy machinery, and dumped them in a nearby lake.

As did Nathan Bedford Forrest a half-century earlier, Evans realized that the ability of Klansmen to hide beneath their hoods encouraged attempting to get away with violence and even murder. So he ordered local leaders to hand over Klan regalia to responsible officers. And rather than take the law into one's own hands, Evans urged Klansmen to work in unison with the local police. After all, it was his fervent hope that those law enforcement agents would join the swelling membership ranks. He believed that by acting as an informant, a Klansman would not only quell the violence that turned the public against the organization, but would also encourage those same policemen to join.

Evans even set out to soften the hateful rhetoric Klansmen had been known to spew about those they considered to be religious, political, or racial enemies, but to little avail. Future president Harry S. Truman was among 45,000 Missourians to join the Klan during its heyday, but after one meeting in which he grew increasingly disgusted by the anti-Catholic speeches, he asked for and received the return of his $10 membership fee.

Few Klan leaders have felt safe in power and Evans was no exception. He feared the fast-rising Stephenson, who had transformed the Indiana Klan into one of the most influential in the nation. Stephenson had become such a force in that state that he was on the verge of buying Valparaiso University, a small college that had run into severe financial hardship. Stephenson awaited backup funds from Klan headquarters in Atlanta, but none arrived. His plan to purchase the school had been destroyed and he placed the blame squarely on Evans, whom he accused of favoring projects in the South while ignoring the North. Stephenson claimed that Evans planned to use national funds to have Klan sympathizer Gutson Borglum, who later created Mount Rushmore, sculpt leading figures of the Confederacy into Stone Mountain. Disagreements between Borglum and Klan leadership killed that project just after the former had begun to chisel away, but Stephenson's complaints were well-founded. After all, Evans had been emphasizing the need for greater Klan influence, which certainly would have been better served by the purchase of a university than a monument to the Confederacy, which hadn't existed in sixty years.

Stephenson's contention that Evans thwarted the plan to purchase Valparaiso based on Northern bias, however, had little merit. Rather, it was predicated on fear. Evans worried that the unprecedented success of Stephenson was a precursor to a rise politically that could actually land the young upstart in the White House. Such a possibility would seem quite unlikely, even in that period of comparative Klan popularity. A Klan leader would have found it quite difficult to land the Republican nomination and earn enough votes to become president. But Evans understood that Stephenson intended to run for a Senate seat in 1926 and worried that the presidency was not out of the realm of possibility. Evans fretted that a President Stephenson would destroy his Klan leadership.

Evans needn't have been concerned. Stephenson couldn't destroy his Klan leadership because he soon set out to destroy himself with his attack on Madge Oberholtzer. What Evans and every Klan leader became alarmed about thereafter was the resulting massive loss of membership. The 1925 march in Washington served only as a last-gasp show of force. By the following year, Evans hoped to regain at least some of that lost popularity by embarking on a speaking tour in 1926, but he was not exactly embraced. Among the greetings he received was expressed sarcastically in Kansas by journalist William Allen White:

> Doctor Hiram Evans, the Imperial Wizard of the Kluxes, is bringing his consecrated shirt tail to Kansas this spring, and from gloomy klaverns will make five Kansas speeches. We welcome him. Enter the Wizard—Sound the bullroarers, and the hewgags. Beat the tom-toms. He will see what was once a thriving and profitable hate factory and bigotorium now laughed into a busted community.[3]

The deterioration of the Klan and its fall from grace came with remarkable rapidity under Evans. An attempt to join the 1927 Memorial Day parade in New York City resulted in disaster as the Boy Scouts and Knights of Columbus withdrew from the festivities on learning that the Klan would be represented. Angry spectators hurled rocks at the marching Klansmen and motorists even tried to run them over. Others managed to battle through policemen who were protecting the group's right to participate in the march and attacked the Klansmen personally.

Although Adolf Hitler and his violently anti-Semitic Nazis found tremendous success playing off the fears and anger of the citizenry to gain power in Germany during the Depression, Evans couldn't inspire the same zeal against the perceived enemies of America during that period. He couldn't stem the tide of anti-Klan feeling and declining membership that bottomed out at about 45,000 by 1930. Evans and his fellow Klansmen led a campaign to discredit Democratic presidential candidate Franklin Roosevelt as a supporter of Catholics and Jews, but to no avail. Roosevelt was swept into office in 1933 and remained there for twelve years.

Soon the terrorists were back in control of the Klan. The Atlanta Klavern launched a series of brutal and fatal floggings later that decade for reasons ranging from premarital sex to a refusal to fire a black employee the Klansmen didn't like. A black barber was stripped naked, whipped, and left to die.

By that time, Evans had already dissolved most Klan property, including the Imperial Palace, due to the financial hardship brought on by the mass defections and the Depression. But Evans was to go out in a blaze of controversy. He sold the Palace to an insurance company that, in turn, sold it to the Roman Catholic Church. Evans was shocked to learn that he had been invited to the dedication ceremony of the new Cathedral of Christ the King in 1939. But to the amazement and anger of his fellow Klansmen, he expressed pleasure at accepting the invitation and indeed met with Catholic priests in the new rectory. Evans later marveled publicly at the beauty of the service.

By that time Evans was toiling for a Georgia construction company. His shady dealings with the Georgia Highway Board cost him $15,000 and he eventually slipped into obscurity. He died in Atlanta in 1966.

NOTES

1. Richard K. Tucker, *The Dragon and the Cross* (Hamden, Conn.: The Shoe String Press, 1991), 5.

2. William G. Shepherd, "The Double Fiery Cross," *Colliers* 82 (July 28, 1928): 9.
3. Charles W. Sloan, "Kansas Battles the Invisible Empire," *Emporia Gazette*, May 15, 1926.

Klansman From Birth: Robert Shelton

Robert Shelton recalled fondly the days and the pageantry of the parades. He embraced the recollections of hundreds upon hundreds white-robed Klansmen waving from the cars in his hometown of Tuscaloosa, Alabama, when he was a child. He recognized some of them as neighbors, and knew that someday he would be donning those same robes.

He would be regaled with stories about the zenith of the KKK during the 1920s from aunts, uncles, and grandparents who had experienced it. He soaked in every word. He was drawn to the Klan world, as other little boys might be attracted to baseball or the adventures of cowboys taming the west. He yearned to follow the same path.

"It gives you kind of a funny feeling, but yet it gives you a feeling of satisfaction, a feeling of desire—desiring to have (a robe) on your-self and become a part of it," Shelton said. "I think actually a person is born a Klansman, and it just works out of him as he develops."[1]

The family ties to the Klan certainly didn't set young Robert apart from the millions of other kids growing up in the segregated South during the Depression—a large percentage of his contempo-raries also boasted one or more Klansmen representing branches of their family trees. His father managed to scrape by financially, pro-viding his family with life's essentials. Robert attended a Methodist church every Sunday and was taught by his parents that blacks and whites simply shouldn't mix, though he was never encouraged to hate. He was led to believe that racial separation, which neither whites nor blacks questioned in Alabama at the time, was both nat-ural and necessary. He gave little thought to the sprinkling of blacks with whom he came into contact in Tuscaloosa.

Shelton gave it far more thought when he was stationed in Ger-many just as President Harry Truman ordered the integration of the armed services. As a result, his racism became more pronounced. His perception that integration would ruin the military led him to what he considered a logical next step, which is that integration would also destroy America. On his return from the service, he began to search for ways to battle the growing call for integration in the United States. He examined his options and decided to join the Ku Klux Klan, an organization he believed best fit his principles and philosophies. The notion of following a family tradition also played a role in his fateful decision.

And indeed, from the time he became a member, the calls for integration in the Jim Crow South were beginning to escalate. In the early 1950s, Shelton joined the Klan that was led by Eldon Edwards. Soon thereafter the Supreme Court *Brown v. Board of Education* decision banned segregation in United States public schools and launched the civil rights movement in earnest. Shelton became associated with the Klan just in time for its third significant era in American history. Since his passion and primary focus of preventing integration matched that of the Klan in the 1950s and 1960s, he rose through the ranks quickly and assumed a position of leadership.

When he returned from the Air Force, Shelton landed a job with the B.F. Goodrich Company, first as a worker in the tire plant and then as a salesman. By that time he had already made his mark with the Klan. In fact, some believe his spearheading the movement to give Klan backing to the election of John Patterson as Alabama governor secured a $1.6 million contract from the state for Goodrich. But Shelton was soon fired, ostensibly for his Klan involvement.

By that time, internal squabbling within the KKK had drastically altered its structure. The 1960 death of Edwards, who had been Imperial Wizard of the dominant U.S. Klans, planted the seeds of change. Successor "Wild Bill" Davidson was deemed unacceptable to Edwards' widow, so Davidson and second-in-command Calvin Craig defected and formed an organization with the expansive title of United Klans, Knights of the Ku Klux Klan of America, Inc., which lured 97 percent of the U.S. Klan membership. Klansmen soon grew disenchanted with Davidson, forcing him to resign. Craig needed a right-hand man and began negotiating with Shelton, who had "distinguished himself" through his role in organizing the beating of dozens of Freedom Riders who had rolled into Montgomery, a feat which earned him an injunction from U.S. Attorney General Robert Kennedy.

Shelton furthered his own cause during a meeting of 500 Klansmen who had poured in from seven Southern states in the aftermath of the attack on the Freedom Riders. The event featured Klansmen from Craig's United Klans, Shelton's independent Alabama Knights, and several splinter groups. It served to unify one and all into a 15,000-Klan organization that called itself the United Klans of America (UKA). He proved to be the undeniable standout during the proceedings. He arrived with an eight-man military guard adorned in white shirts, red ties, khaki paratrooper pants, black boots, marine helmets and bayonets fixed to their white belts. He was expressing his fervent desire to do battle against the civil rights movement and the rapidly liberalizing leaders in Washington who were threatening the so-called Southern way of life. Shelton so impressed his fellow Klansmen that he was named Imperial Wizard of the UKA by proclamation. In fact, they even voted to transfer the headquarters of the UKA from Atlanta to Shelton's hometown of Tuscaloosa.

In 1961, the thirty-two-year-old Shelton was suddenly the youngest man ever thrust into his position of power, which is the same that could be said about new President John F. Kennedy. Though a man of little outward emotion and not one to warm up a room with a smile, he was unafraid to speak to the media. And unlike Klan leaders of the past such as Simmons and Evans, he openly expressed his intense racism and anti-Semitism. He spewed offerings such as a belief that full moons prompted blacks to become more violent due to their "animal instincts," and that "it is very dangerous to hire (blacks), especially a babysitter (because) all they have to do is cut their finger, drop a drop of blood in the baby's food and it will be dead within a year from sickle cell anemia." He also said, "I don't hate niggers, but I hate the Jews. The nigger's a child, but the Jews are dangerous people. . . . All they want is control and domination of the Gentiles through a conspiracy with the niggers." Shelton also claimed that all Jews were by nature Communistic.[2]

Shelton sprang into action, using his militancy and seriousness in going about his business to launch the most violent period in the history of the Klan. Such seminal events of the civil rights movement such as the church bombing that killed four black children in Birmingham, the murders of the three civil rights workers in

Mississippi, the killings of Reverend James Reeb and Viola Liuzzo in Selma, and the shooting death of Colonel Lemuel Penn in Georgia occurred during Shelton's reign. The Justice Department concluded that between 1954 and 1966, a period in which Shelton was heavily involved in and eventually directed Klan activities, the KKK was responsible for nearly seventy bombings in Georgia and Alabama, thirty church burnings in Mississippi, and dozens of lynchings.

Shelton solidified the Klan through three strong lieutenants who served as Grand Dragons in their respective states—Calvin Craig (Georgia), Robert Scoggin (South Carolina), and Bob Jones (North Carolina), who proved the most effective of all in building up membership. By 1966, the North Carolina Klan boasted 192 Klaverns and nearly 7,500 members.

The civil rights movement had given the Klan a mission, but Shelton provided a feeling of unity. During his tenure as Imperial Wizard that began with the consolidation, there were few changes in the Klan hierarchy. He expanded the organization into more than thirty states, several of which had been dormant in terms of Klan activity since the 1930s. And though it was never proven that Shelton was personally involved in the killings associated with the civil rights movement, he verbally backed Klansmen accused of and eventually indicted for those murders. He even helped organize parades and rallies honoring Sheriff Lawrence Rainey and Deputy Cecil Price, two Klansmen who were eventually jailed after the killings of the three civil rights workers in Mississippi. Shelton also downplayed the shooting of Liuzzo, questioning her moral character with claims of a police record and her relationship with her husband. He added that she belonged back in Milwaukee taking care of her kids. Shelton even took the witness stand in the defense of Klansmen who were charged with Liuzzo's murder. When the trial ended in a hung jury, those Klansmen, too, were celebrated during Klan events.

In the early 1960s, Shelton had hitched his wagon to rising political star George Wallace, whom Shelton enthusiastically supported in both gubernatorial and presidential bids. In 1964, when Wallace set off on his first of two completed bids for the presidency (he was shot and wounded during the 1972 campaign, which prematurely ended that attempt), Shelton met with fellow Klansman

Asa Carter in Indiana to help plan the Wallace strategy. Carter was infamous for heading the Klan in Birmingham in 1957 when six of its members castrated a black handyman in what was considered one of the most shocking race-related crimes in American history. So brutal was the mutilation that an Alabama court, all of which had been notorious for allowing Klansmen to walk free no matter how nefarious the act, found the perpetrators guilty before a judge sentenced them to twenty years in prison. Wallace paroled them when he became governor of Alabama. Shelton understood that Wallace was the Klan's best friend. The governor even praised the Klan in an interview, stating that in 1967 while race riots and antiwar protests were tearing the nation apart, "At least a Klansman will fight for his country. He don't tear up his draft card. But the Klan, it's just innocuous in size and they're concerned with segregation, not subversiveness."[3]

Neither Shelton nor any other Klan leader, however, could stem the tide of the civil rights movement. By the early 1970s, though still Imperial Wizard of the UKA, which still boasted the largest membership of any Klan organization, Shelton had taken a job as a used car dealer to survive financially. He was also falling out of favor while David Duke became the new darling of many Klansmen.

Speaking in 1976, when such issues as affirmative action and busing had raised the ire of many in white America, Shelton claimed that the events of the 1960s required violence. "There was a certain amount of hostility and violence involved [in the 1960s]," he admitted. "After all, you were doing a complete one eighty turn in your society. It's unfortunate, really, that there wasn't more violence than what it was. I feel like had there been enough violence, it would have stopped all this, and we wouldn't be in the position we're in today. . . . There's still going to be a revolution. There's got to. There's no way to prevent it. We're witnessing job discrimination in reverse."[4]

Shelton remained active with the UKA until the $7 million lawsuit filed by the mother of slain black teenager Michael Donald brought down the organization. Thereafter, he lived in secrecy near Tuscaloosa and died on March 19, 2003, at the age of seventy-three.

Following Shelton's death, Morris Dees, who founded the Southern Poverty Law Center that filed the lawsuit that destroyed the UKA, expressed his belief that the former Imperial Wizard was an evil man. Dees added that the violent acts perpetrated by the Klan in the 1960s could not have been carried out without Shelton's approval or perhaps even his complicity.

But the man who seemed to be born a Klansman died as one as well. He told a reporter in the mid-1990s that the Klan was both his belief and his religion, though he conceded that the organization no longer served a purpose and would never return to a position of strength.

NOTES

1. Patsy Sims, *The Klan* (Lexington, Ky.: The University Press of Kentucky, 1996), 93.
2. Margaret Long, "The Imperial Wizard Explains the Klan," *New York Times Magazine*, July 5, 1964, 8, 25–26.
3. Tom Wicker, "A Gross and Simple Heart," *Harper's*, April 1967, 41–49.
4. Sims, *The Klan*, 95.

Mr. Klean: David Duke

The common belief is that racism is learned on daddy's knee. David Duke was certainly an exception. His father even warned him not to join any far right-wing organizations before his son left for his freshman year at Louisiana State University (LSU) in 1968. Duke's upbringing didn't fit that of the typical Klansman. He was indeed raised in the South, but lived in various locations. However, he suffered through none of the financial and educational inadequacies of so many of his predecessors that motivated them to join the organization.

Though he was born in Tulsa, Duke's family later lived in Europe, and he attended kindergarten in The Hague before his family moved back to the United States. He was sent to a private military school in Georgia and later lived in New Orleans. His father, an engineer for Shell Oil, stressed the importance of education and forced his son to read for at least one hour every day. The younger Duke, whose grandmother was a chemistry professor at the University of Kansas, was particularly adept at and taken with science. He devoured magazines such as *Popular Mechanics* and *Science*

Digest every month and considered himself destined for a career as an anthropologist, archeologist, or biologist.

His mindset changed dramatically at age twelve when he read the book, *Race and Reason: A Yankee View,* by Carleton Putnam that espoused segregation. The book was published in 1961 during the height of the civil rights movement, but it presented a far more thoughtful and intellectual viewpoint on the subject than did the Klansmen who at the time responded to the growing call for integration by blowing up churches and lynching blacks. Duke claims to have even been leaning toward liberalism before poring over the Putnam work, which, though it didn't change his mind entirely about race relations, did plant the seeds for his future segregationist stand.

It was at that time Duke began to believe that race was the most important element to the survival of modern civilization and the betterment of American society. Although he has maintained his claim that he has never been a white supremacist, his stated view that what is most important in the world is the quality of people and that he feared the white race was being overcome by the non-white races might lead one to believe otherwise.

It was with growing right-wing radicalism that he arrived at LSU. Aside from the year off from college during which he taught English to local Laotians in a project run by the State Department, Duke became involved both privately and publicly in far right-wing activities. He studied white supremacy, anti-Semitism, and Nazi history and joined Louisiana's independent Knights of the Ku Klux Klan. During the early 1970s, however, few KKK groups, even in the South, were flourishing. And the Louisiana Knights were certainly no exception. In fact, Duke was among the older members during his college days. The Louisiana Knights boasted mostly high school kids who did little more than meet and vent. He was easily able to take over the local organization after his graduation from college.

Duke had gained experience as an organizer at LSU. He formed a chapter of the White Youth Alliance, which he managed to spread to forty other universities, most of which resided in the South. The Alliance wasn't particularly active, however. Its main function was to distribute racist literature, including Duke's own newsletter, to fellow students. But Duke did grab some attention when, dressed like a Nazi storm-trooper and wearing a swastika armband, he protested a speech by left-wing attorney William Kunstler by marching with a placard that read GAS THE CHICAGO SEVEN, a group of defendants that had been indicted for allegedly starting a riot at the 1968 Democratic Convention. The stunt not only earned him the rather undesirable title of "the Nazi of LSU," but it also gave him a reputation as a full-fledged Nazi. Some of the pamphlets and newsletters he passed out were even produced by the American Nazi Party.

That image attracted the National Socialist White People's Party (NSWPP). Its official publication touted Duke as a National Socialist leader at LSU. Duke then copied passages from a NSWPP pamphlet verbatim and placed it in a White Student Alliance membership application. Duke later claimed that such actions could be attributed to youthful exuberance and that he regretted only that others mistook them for showing sympathy for Nazism.

The liberalization of America in the 1960s and early 1970s along with the reputation of the Klan as a rabidly violent organization sent its membership spiraling downward considerably. Its leaders were grasping for anyone who could revive it, but it appeared the old-style Klan was gone forever. Even though he had graduated from LSU just a year earlier, Duke was considered by some as a Klan savior who could lead an organization that appeared to be on death's door into a new era. Many of its leaders struggled to comprehend the next generation dressed spiffily in a suit and tie rather than in a white hood and robe, but they were in no position to look a gift leader in the mouth.

Duke blamed the media for causing the Klan to be reviled, but he also understood that lynching and church bombings were no way to tug at the heartstrings of Americans. Though he donned a white robe at rallies, he never wore a hood and he courted the media dressed conservatively. He recruited on college campuses and attempted to lure more intellectual, educated members. He opened the Patriot Bookstore in Metairie, Louisiana, which sold not only racist books and paraphernalia that were typically linked to the Klan, but also intellectually oriented books that espoused white supremacy and white separatism. He even welcomed Catholics into his Knights and both his charm and good looks naturally appealed to women. Duke professed non-violence and never uttered incendiary racist or anti-Semitic words or phrases. Like Wesley Hiram Evans two generations earlier, he believed that the way to further the Klan cause was through politics.

The same media he chastised for sending Americans what he perceived to be the wrong message about the Klan followed him around with greater interest than they had for any other previous KKK leader. He quickly became a curiosity as the man who had single-handedly destroyed the image of Klansmen that had been cemented in the vision and minds of Americans for more than a century. Rather than angrily spewing radical right-wing views as Klan leaders had typically done since the 1930s, Duke calmly attempted to further the cause by expressing himself articulately and without rancor. As Knights National Information Director in 1973, he appeared on national television talk shows and embarked on a college speaking tour. Though some Klansmen criticized him and claimed he was simply publicizing himself through an infatuation with media attention, others welcomed the new approach.

Klan leader David Duke, age twenty-seven, poses in his Klan robes in front of the House of Parliament in London, 1978. Although he was banned from entering Britain, he arrived by way of a Skytrain flight from New York. Source: *AP Photo.*

Duke envisioned the White Knights of the Ku Klux Klan under his leadership as boasting the same non-violent and populist tendencies of the KKK in the 1920s, but he also believed its philosophies mirrored that of its founders during the Reconstruction period. He felt that the group in the early part of the century focused far too much on promoting the social rather than the political aspects of participation. He espoused the White Knights as a force for positive change for the white race in America, which he added was not the same motivation of the United Klans of America and other splinter groups.

Duke claimed that any movement for social change must be achieved inside, not outside, the American system. He announced that the Klan would be openly running candidates for political office. And he spoke with disdain about those who would typecast Klansmen as little more than ignorant, discourteous, tobacco-chewing hillbillies.

Duke's plans were working. The Knights grew into a national organization with 3,500 members, which included organizations in states with liberal reputations such as Connecticut, New York, and California. When Duke began his foray into political campaigning, he named Bill Wilkinson as his successor as Louisiana Grand Dragon. The move backfired when Wilkinson quit and formed the independent Invisible Empire, Knights of the Ku Klux Klan, which lured away most of Duke's Knights.

Duke not only lost members to the Invisible Empire, but also was unable to convince Wilkinson to curb Klan violence; this combination of events motivated Duke to launch the National Association for the Advancement of White People (NAAWP). He assured Wilkinson that since the fledgling NAAWP would appeal to people in a higher socio-economic class, it wouldn't cut into Klan membership. Duke then privately offered to sell Wilkinson the Knights membership list for $35,000. Not only did Wilkinson refuse—he didn't need the list because most of Duke's members were heading in his direction anyway—but he also secretly taped the conversation and turned the recording over to the media. The news that Duke had sold out his members did little damage to his reputation, but the NAAWP still flopped miserably and remained dead in the water five years after launching.

In 1985, he spoke with doctoral student Evelyn Rich, who traveled the country with Duke while researching the KKK for her dissertation. Duke held little back about his views on racial separatism.

> What we really want to do is to be left alone. We don't want Negroes around. We don't need Negroes around. We're not asking— you know, we don't want to have them, you know, for our culture. We simply want our own country and our own society. That's in no way exploitive at all. We want our own society, our own nation. . ."[1]

Duke also struggled politically. He lost several bids for state and U.S. Senate seats, as well as for governor of Louisiana, and even ran two barely-visible campaigns for president, first as a Democrat in 1988 and then as a Populist Party candidate in 1992.

After another unsuccessful bid to earn a spot in the U.S. Senate in 1996, Duke shed his comparatively moderate image and went on the attack against blacks and Jews. He penned a 700-page autobiography titled *My Awakening* in which he attempted to prove that whites were genetically superior to blacks and devoted 250 pages to anti-Semitic rhetoric.

In 2000, Duke formed the National Organization for European American Rights, which he claimed would serve the rights of whites in America that the National Association for the Advancement of Colored People (NAACP) had for blacks. That same year he traveled to Russia to speak to ultranationalists and called for increased anti-Zionist sentiment and the banishment of all dark-skinned people in Moscow. He received a rousing ovation.

At about that time, federal agents raided Duke's home in Mandeville, Louisiana. The search warrant was issued based on informants that claimed Duke had taken hundreds of thousands of dollars from supporters and gambled the money away at casinos. In 2002, Duke was also indicted for mail fraud and filing a false tax return, for which he was convicted and received fifteen months in prison.

On his release in 2004, Duke came out on the side of liberals and the growing number of protesters after the terrorist attacks on New York on September 11, 2001, and the launching of the war in Iraq. But his opposing view was based on quite different reasons than those of most fostering antiwar sentiment. He lashed out against the war because of his perception that it served only Israel. And in 2006, Duke spoke at the Holocaust Conference in Tehran, Iran, during which he didn't deny the Holocaust, but used the word "alleged" in reference to the severity of the German systematic massacre of Jews during World War II. He also stated his belief that Americans were fighting the wrong enemy in the Middle East:

> Let me say from the outset that I am no disloyal American, I love my country and my people, but I know that the Zionist extremists lead my country to catastrophe in the Mideast and elsewhere around the world. I know that the Palestinian people, the Lebanese people, even the American people have been sacrificed on the altar of the Holocaust. It is the chronic media and government playing of the Holocaust that has blinded our eyes to new holocausts and new outrages.
>
> As a truly patriotic American I oppose Americans being killed or maimed by the thousands in Iraq in a war not for America, but for Israel. I am here because I love my country and oppose those who lead America and the world to ruin on behalf of Zionism. In Iraq too, Americans and countless Iraqis have been sacrificed on the ideological altar of the Holocaust, for the Holocaust and its chronic recital is used as the justification of any Israeli treachery or crime against humanity.[2]

The rise to power of Barack Obama as the first African American president also raised the ire of Duke, who considered it a dark day for the nation. "I believe tonight is a night of tragedy and sadness for our people in many ways," Duke said on an Internet radio program. "The country is not recognizable any more."[3]

Duke was barely recognizable anymore either to millions of Americans. Few were paying attention to what he had to say by that time. Just like every Klan leader of the past, he had fallen out of the spotlight and into obscurity. The difference was that after Duke left the Klan, the Klan, too, fell into obscurity.

NOTES

1. Anti-Defamation League, "Extremism in America, Evelyn Rich Interview, March 1985." http://www.adl.org/Learn/Ext_US/duke.asp (accessed February 4, 2009).
2. David Duke, "David Duke Delivers Speech in Tehran; Calls for Free Speech on Holocaust Issue," November 11, 2006. http://www.davidduke.com/general/david-duke-delivers-speech-in-tehran-calls-for-free-speech-on-the-holocaust-issue_1532.html (accessed February 4, 2009).
3. Anti-Defamation League, "White Supremacist Rage Boils over after Obama Victory; Racist Site Crashes after Election," November 10, 2008. http://www.adl.org/PresRele/Extremism_72/5387_72.htm (accessed February 4, 2009).

The Next Generation: Tom Metzger

Tom Metzger was not just any TV repairman. He had assumed leadership in the John Birch Society, Ku Klux Klan, White American Political Association, and White Aryan Resistance; won a California Democratic Congressional primary; spearheaded the American neo-Nazi skinhead movement; spent forty-five days in jail; been involved with brawls and riots; refused to pay taxes during the Vietnam War; and held negotiations with, of all groups, the New Black Panther Party.

Metzger was born and raised in a Catholic home in Warsaw, Indiana, and was considered a likeable fellow with an interest in science. He began compiling his extensive and broad-based résumé in 1961. The former army corporal who had moved to California to forge a career in electronics, decided to expand his horizons. An avowed racist and anti-Semite, he joined the John Birch Society. He also served as a precinct worker on the 1964 presidential campaign of Republican Barry Goldwater, who lost in a landslide to Lyndon Johnson. Four years later he threw his support to independent George Wallace, who finished a distant third to Richard Nixon and Hubert Humphrey.

By that time, Metzger had left the John Birch Society, stating that the organization didn't give him enough freedom to criticize Jews. He searched for an outlet for his radical right-wing views until deciding in 1975 to hook up with the Knights of the Ku Klux Klan founded by David Duke, who took little time naming him Grand Dragon of California.

Metzger brandished a .45 Colt pistol, even outside his home, and introduced black uniforms rather than white robes for his members. He used his skills in electronics to create a computerized enemies list and a complex video surveillance system over his San Diego home. Highly political, he attracted publicity for the California Klan by leading a very visible protest of the influx of Vietnamese boat people in San Diego. His group picketed against the immigrants before marching to the federal courthouse. Metzger latched on tightly to the immigration issue, organizing a patrol of armed Klansmen to capture Mexicans illegally crossing over the American border in 1979. Immigration commissioner L. J. Castillo deemed that citizens' arrests of that nature were illegal, but Metzger continued to arm his Klansmen. They engaged in clashes against anti-Klan protesters and the police. In the spring of 1980, he led thirty armed Klan members against anti-Klan protesters in Oceanside, California, in a battle that resulted in seven people being injured.

Several weeks later, Metzger broke free from Duke to make his California Klan independent. He also followed Duke's lead by setting his sights on political office. Metzger shocked many by garnering 33,000 votes in winning the California Democratic Congressional primary. But in a rare move, the state's Democratic Party disavowed its candidate for his espoused racism and anti-Semitism and urged voters to select Republican Clair Burgener. The result was a landslide—Burgener received 253,949 votes to Metzger's 35,107. Metzger did recruit young members into his Klan during the campaign, however, stating along the way that elementary and secondary schools should provide classes in how to handle guns.

Metzger abandoned the Klan later that year to form the White American Political Association (WAPA) in an attempt to promote "pro-white" candidates. Among those candidates was Metzger himself, who ran in the 1982 California Democratic primary and fared miserably, earning less than 3 percent of the vote. His inability to make the WAPA or his own political career thrive motivated him to leave politics and transform his organization into the White American Resistance, which later morphed into the White Aryan Resistance (WAR). It was in that capacity that Metzger gained his greatest notoriety. He spread his message of hate in the *White Aryan Resistance* monthly newsletter, which copied such publications of the past such as *Der Sturmer* in Nazi Germany by featuring exaggerated and grotesque cartoons of Jews and blacks in an attempt to further racist and anti-Semitic views.

Metzger expanded his reach in 1984 with a videotaped series he produced for cable TV stations titled *Race and Reason*. The show revolved around Metzger's interviews of leaders of racist and anti-Semitic organizations and was distributed around the country. Small cable stations in major cities aired the program. Metzger created one hundred fifty such programs, which gained him enough publicity to land guest appearances on talk shows such as *The Geraldo Rivera Show*, on which in November 1988 he showed up with son John Metzger and several neo-Nazi skinheads to confront an African American activist. The result was a brawl before a national television audience in which Rivera received a broken nose from a thrown chair.

In fact, Metzger was considered the father of the racist skinhead movement. He was the first to effectively use the growing power of computers to spread propaganda and provide an outlet for racist youth. He set up a rudimentary computerized list of announcements of meetings planned by the Klan and other racist organizations. He targeted young people and, in fact, in January 1985 distributed several hundred thousand flyers to students in California claiming that the Holocaust was a hoax.

It call came crashing down for Metzger in November 1988, when skinheads representing the East Side White Pride in Portland, Oregon, savagely beat three Ethiopian immigrants with a baseball bat and steel-toed boots. One of the victims was killed. The investigation revealed a close tie between the skinheads, all of whom received convictions, and the WAR. The Southern Poverty and Anti-Defamation League (ADL) sued Metzger on behalf of the family of murdered immigrant, Mulugeta Seraw. The connection between the skinheads and Metzger was confirmed by a letter to the skinheads signed by Metzger stating that WAR national vice-president Dave Mazzella would be traveling to Portland to instruct them on the proper methods of attack. Mazzella did indeed carry out the mission and later admitted that "Tom Metzger said the only way to get respect from skinheads is to teach them how to commit violence against blacks, against Jews, Hispanics, any minority. The word will spread, and they will know our group is one you can respect."[1]

Mazzella later repented, calling the ADL to formally renounce his racist beliefs and his ties with Metzger. He proved to be a key witness for the prosecution and played a role in the $12.5 million in damages awarded to the Seraw family. The judgment forced WAR to pay $5 million, followed by John Metzger ($4 million), and Tom Metzger ($3 million). The other $500,000 would be paid by two of the murderers. It was among the largest judgments of its kind in American history. Metzger's assets, including his home, were seized. Though WAR certainly couldn't pay the entire amount immediately, its subsequent revenues were liquidated and a high percentage of its profits sent to the Seraw family.

The law continued to hound Metzger. Among his money-making schemes was selling T-shirts featuring the popular cartoon character Bart Simpson wearing a Nazi uniform with the words "Pure Nazi Dude" and "Total Nazi Dude" on them. Metzger was pressured to stop that venture and later that year was found guilty of unlawful assembly stemming from a cross-burning incident in Los Angeles in 1983. He was sent to jail, but his six-month sentence was commuted to just forty-six days so he could attend to his sick wife, Kathleen, who died in March 1992. Although Metzger was ordered to remain in the United States and contribute 300 hours of community service during that time, he left for Canada. The Canadian government soon deported him back to American authorities after he attempted to organize and speak at a rally of the radically right-wing Heritage Home Front organization in Toronto.

Soon Metzger was advocating what became known as the "lone wolf" method of spreading extremist ideology. This influential philosophy forwarded the notion that the failure to change society over the previous three decades was the result of easy identification of organizations touting white supremacy or white separatism. He furthered the concept created by past neo-Nazi and Klan leader Louis Beam, who believed individual racists should act alone or in very small groups when taking violent measures against political enemies.

Among those one would consider a political enemy that Metzger attempted to befriend was the New Black Panther Party (NBPP). The organization was founded in 1989, a generation after the original Black Panther Party reached its peak as a militant group espousing black power in the 1960s. Metzger spoke to the group in 1993 about what he perceived to be common goals, including separatism and anti-Semitism, which the NBPP had embraced. Metzger has also claimed his openness to establishing an alliance with controversial Louis Farrakhan and the radical Nation of Islam to forward those same causes. Though nothing became of those rather unusual and shocking forays into creating relationships with radical black groups, Metzger continued to espouse his racist and anti-Semitic rhetoric on an Internet program titled *Insurgent Radio*.

There was, however, another side to Metzger's worldview. He railed against capitalism, large corporations, and every entanglement in which Americans have been involved since the Civil War. He would sound like a left-winger as he criticized the government for its actions in Korea, Vietnam, and Iraq, as well as attempts by Republicans and right-wing advocates for what he considered an attempt to destroy the labor movement in the United States. The difference is that his opinions were based on a perceived racial struggle.

Metzger had become no less vigilant as Barack Obama campaigned for the presidency in 2008. But again he took what one might consider a surprising stand about the possibility of the first black president to take office in the United States. One week before the election he said the following:

> The corporations are running things now, so it's not going to make much difference who's in there, but [Republican candidate John McCain] would be much worse. He's a warmonger. He's a scary, scary person—more dangerous than [President George W. Bush]. Obama. . . . is a racist and I have no problem with black racists. I don't hate black people. I just think it's in the best interest of the races to be separated as much as possible. See, I'm a leftist. I'm not a rightist. I hate the transnational corporations far more than any black person.[2]

One might believe that if he had told that to three racist skinheads in 1988, one Ethiopian immigrant might be alive today.

NOTES

1. The Nizkor Project, "Tom Metzger's Long March of Hate," June 1993. Available at: http://www.nizkor.org/ftp.cgi/orgs/american/adl/tom-metzger/adl-metzger (Accessed February 8, 2009).

2. David Peisner, "Why White Supremacists Support Barack Obama," *Esquire Magazine* online, October 30, 2008. http://www.esquire.com/the-side/feature/racists-support-obama-061308 (accessed February 9, 2009).

Appendix: Significant Klan Leaders

Until the Klan had been thoroughly weakened and splintered and other more militaristic right-wing organizations captured the imagination and attention of radical racists in the 1980s, the organization was generally run by one powerful leader.

The following is a short list of the Grand Wizards, Imperial Wizards, and other leaders who led the KKK for well more than a century:

1865–1868   John C. Lester: Knight Hawk
             J. R. Crowe: Grand Turk
             John Kennedy: Grand Maji
             Frank McCord: Grand Cyclops

1867–1869   Nathan Bedford Forrest: Grand Wizard

1915–1923   William Joseph Simmons: Imperial Wizard

1923–1939   Hiram Wesley Evans: Imperial Wizard

1939–1944   James Colescott: Imperial Wizard

1946–1949   Samuel Green: Imperial Wizard

1949–1950   Samuel Roper: Imperial Wizard

1950–1960   Eldon Edwards: Imperial Wizard

1960–1987   Robert Shelton: Imperial Wizard, United Klans of America

1974–1978   David Duke: National Director, National Knights of the Ku Klux Klan

1975–1983   Bill Wilkinson: Imperial Wizard, Invisible Empire, Knights of the Ku Klux Klan

Glossary of Klan Terms

The Pulaski Six not only founded the Klan in 1865, but a new language as well. Though dozens of terms to describe KKK officials, organizations, groups, and ceremonies have been added over the years, the original Klansmen launched a separate vocabulary with interesting and colorful terminology.

It should be noted that the titles for all Klan officers and aides exist on national, state, and province levels. The names are prefaced with "Imperial" on the national level, "Grand" on the state level, and "Great" on the province level.

The following is a list of Klan terms and abbreviations.

AKIA: A password translated into "A Klansman I am," which can be sometimes seen on Klan bumper stickers and other paraphernalia.

Alien: Any non-Klansman.

AYAK?: A password translated into "Are You a Klansman?"

Banish: To revoke membership for any one of many offenses, generally following a trial in front of a Klan tribunal.

CLASP: A password translated into "Clannish Loyalty a Sacred Principle."

Exalted Cyclops: President or leader of a local Klavern, often referred to as "E.C."

Furies: All officers of Klan provinces aside from Great Titans.

Genii: The collective title of all national Klan officers who serve as advisors to the Imperial Wizard.

Ghouls: Now rarely used term for all rank-and-file Klansmen.

Grand Dragon: Top state Klan officer.

Grand Giant: Formerly the top state Klan officer.

Great Titan: Leader of a province or congressional district.

Hydras: All Realm officers not including the Grand Dragon.

Imperial: The title preface to all national officers.

Imperial Giant: Formerly the Imperial Wizard.

Imperial Klonvocation: The national convention.

Imperial Wizard: The national Klan leader.

Inner Circle: A small group of Klan members who create and carry out generally a violent plan of action against an individual or group, such as a cross burning, bombing, or lynching. The plan and action remain a secret to all other Klan members, which serves to prevent fellow Klansmen from leaking facts to authorities and becoming legally involved. This also limits the search for perpetrators and accomplices.

Invisible Empire: The overall geographical entity "served" by the Klan, such as the United States, even when no Klavern exists in particular states.

Kalendar: The Klan calendar, which traces events from its Reconstruction beginnings and its 1915 rebirth. It is broken up into months called Bloody, Gloomy, Hideous, Fearful, Furious, Alarming, Terrible, Horrible, Mournful, Sorrowful, Frightful and Appalling. The weeks on the Kalendar are known as Woeful, Weeping, Wailing, Wonderful, and Weird, while the days are listed as Dark, Deadly, Dismal, Doleful, Desolate, Dreadful, and Desperate.

Kardinal Kullors: The official primary Klan colors of crimson, gold, and black and secondary colors of gray, green, and blue. The Imperial Wizard's Kullor is "royal" purple.

K.B.I.: The Klan Bureau of Investigation.

KIGY!: A password translated into, "Klansman, I Greet You!"

KKKK: Knight of the Ku Klux Klan, which became the group's official title since its 1915 revival.

Klabee: Klan treasurer.

Kladd: Conductor of Klan ceremonies.

Klaliff: Vice-President of a Klavern or elsewhere in the Klan hierarchy.

Klan Giant: Honorary title given to a still-respected former Exalted Cyclops.

Klankraft: The philosophies and practices of the Klan.

Klanton: The jurisdiction of an individual Klavern.

Klarogo: The inner Klavern guard.

Klavern: A local Klan group, otherwise known as a "den."

Kleagle: A Klan organizer in charge of growing membership who in some organizations receives a percentage of all initiation fees.

Klectokon: The initiation fee, most often $15, generally split between Klavern and state and national Klan offices. Annual Klan dues have most often run between $24 and $36.

Klepper: An elected Imperial Klonvocation delegate.

Klexter: The outer Klavern guard.

Kligrapp: Klan secretary.

Klokan: The head of the three-man Klokan Board, which votes on candidates for membership and also serves as auditor.

Klokard: One who lectures about and teaches Klan philosophy.

Kloncilium: The advisory board to the Imperial Wizard, otherwise known as Genii.

Klonkave: Secret Klan meeting.

Kloran: Official Klan book explaining its rituals.

Klolero: Realm convention.

Kludd: Klan chaplain.

Night Hawk: Responsible for the fiery cross and for candidates for Klan membership immediately prior to initiation. Responsible in some Klan organizations for finding victims of violence and most often dressed in black robe.

Province: A subdivision of a Realm, sometimes divided into congressional districts.

Realm: A subdivision of the Invisible Empire, often divided into states.

Realm Tax: The percentage of initiation fees and annual dues sent to individual state headquarters.

SAN BOG: The password given to Klansmen warning that "Strangers Are Near, Be on Guard."

Splinter groups: Organizations that claim the "Knights of the Ku Klux Klan" title but are unaffiliated and are most often founded and run by disenchanted former Klansmen.

Terrors: Exalted Cyclops' officers, which include a Klaliff, Klokard, Kludd, Kligrapp, Klabee, Kladd, Klarogo, Klexter, Klokan, and Night Hawk.

Primary Documents
The Klan in "Black and White"

The relationship between the Ku Klux Klan and the media has changed with the times. That's not to imply that the KKK has changed with the times—at least not dramatically. The racist, anti-Semitic, and anti-immigrant beliefs and actions that have defined the organization since Reconstruction have stayed as consistent as one could possibly imagine considering the transformation of American society over that same period. But that very transformation has also resulted in a drastic shift in how the media has viewed and reported on the Klan over the past 150 years.

One might argue that the Klan has gone through times in which its rhetoric softened and its members managed to tone down its violence during its heyday from 1915 to 1925 to lure new members and attract more positive media attention. But the white supremacist and separatist philosophy of the Klan and the violent and even murderous tactics it has used in an attempt to achieve its aims have remained virtually unchanged. As American society and therefore the mainstream media have grown more tolerant, both have distanced themselves and become more critical of the Klan. It can also be suggested that the lack of violent activity in more recent years has been due greatly to the fact that the organization has all but ceased to exist on the American political radar.

I. The Foundation

What many believe to be the hypocrisy of the stated Klan purpose as it relates to its actions can be found in the claimed principles the organization set forth in 1868. Note in the following that the objects of the original Klan was to protect the weak, innocent, and defenseless from the violent and brutal and to relieve the oppressed. However, no group of people in the South at that time was weaker and more oppressed than the just-freed slaves and no organization showed greater brutality toward them than the Klan itself. The belief that blacks shouldn't gain social or political equality was even a prerequisite to gaining membership.

The Appellation states strongly that the Klan recognizes the sanctity and righteousness of the Constitution, yet it set out to destroy every Constitutional mandate regarding the rights of fellow men.

Appellation

This organization shall be styled and denominated the Order of the___We, the Order of the ___, reverentially acknowledge the majesty and supremacy of the Divine Being and recognize the goodness and providence of the same. And we recognize our relation to the United States government, the supremacy of the Constitution, the constitutional laws thereof, and the Union of states thereunder.

Character and Objects of the Order

This is an institution of chivalry, humanity, mercy, and patriotism; embodying in its genius and its principles all that is chivalric in conduct, noble in sentiment, generous in manhood, and patriotic in purpose; its peculiar objects being:

First, to protect the weak, the innocent, and the defenseless from the indignities, wrongs, and outrages of the lawless, the violent, and the brutal; to relieve the injured and oppressed; to succor the suffering and unfortunate, and especially the widows and orphans of Confederate soldiers.

Second, to protect and defend the Constitution of the United States, and all laws passed in conformity thereto, and to protect the states and the people thereof from all invasion from any source whatever.

Third, to aid and assist in the execution of all constitutional laws, and to protect the people from unlawful seizure and from trial, except by their peers in conformity to the laws of the land.

Titles

Section 1. The officers of this Order shall consist of a Grand Wizard of the Empire and his ten Genii; a Grand Dragon of the Realm and his eight Hydras; a Grand Titan of the Dominion and his six Furies; a Grand Giant of the Province and his four Goblins; a Grand Cyclops of the Den and his two Night Hawks; a Grand Magi, a Grand Monk, a Grand Scribe, a Grand Exchequer, a Grand Turk, and a Grand Sentinel.

Section 2. The body politic of this Order shall be known and designated as "Ghouls."

Territory and Its Divisions

Section 1. The territory embraced within the jurisdiction of this Order shall be coterminous with the states of Maryland, Virginia, North Carolina, South Carolina, Georgia, Florida, Alabama, Mississippi, Louisiana, Texas, Arkansas, Missouri, Kentucky, and Tennessee; all combined constituting the Empire.

Section 2. The Empire shall be divided into four departments, the first to be styled the Realm and coterminous with the boundaries of the several states; the second to be styled the Dominion and to be coterminous with such counties as the Grand Dragons of the several Realms may assign to the charge of the Grand Titan. The third to be styled the Province and to be coterminous with the several counties; provided, the Grand Titan may, when he deems it necessary, assign two Grand Giants to one Province, prescribing, at the same time, the jurisdiction of each. The fourth department to be styled the Den, and shall embrace such part of a Province as the Grand Giant shall assign to the charge of a Grand Cyclops.

Questions to Be Asked Candidates

1. Have you ever been rejected, upon application for membership in the ___, or have you ever been expelled from the same?
2. Are you now, or have you ever been a member of the Radical Republican Party, or either of the organizations known as the "Loyal League" and the "Grand Army of the Republic"?
3. Are you opposed to the principles and policy of the Radical Party, and to the Loyal League, and the Grand Army of the Republic, so far as you are informed of the character and purposes of those organizations?
4. Did you belong to the Federal Army during the late war, and fight against the South during the existence of the same?
5. Are you opposed to Negro equality both social and political?
6. Are you in favor of a white man's government in this country?
7. Are you in favor of constitutional liberty, and a government of equitable laws instead of a government of violence and oppression?
8. Are you in favor of maintaining the constitutional rights of the South?
9. Are you in favor of the reenfranchisement and emancipation of the white men of the South, and the restitution of the Southern people to all their rights, alike proprietary, civil, and political?
10. Do you believe in the inalienable right of self-preservation of the people against the exercise of arbitrary and unlicensed power?

Source: "Organization and Principles of the Ku Klux Klan, 1868," State University of New York at Albany. http://www.albany.edu/faculty/gz580/his101/kkk.html (accessed February 13, 2009).

2. Terrorizing Kids

By the time Nathan Bedford Forrest gained leadership of the Ku Klux Klan in 1867, mere intimidation of blacks and political enemies had given way to terror and murder. In some cases, it was difficult to distinguish between Klan intimidation and terror.

The growth of Klan membership left its leadership unable to control individual ghouls. The Klan was no longer centralized in Tennessee. It

spread to other Southern states, including South Carolina. One example of
a Klan act that teetered between intimidation and terror occurred in the
summer of 1868 and was described in the following article published in
the Charleston Courier.

During the latter part of last week a rumor became widespread among the colored people of Charleston, and among many of the whites, which, for a time, produced much consternation. We have been at some trouble to investigate the matter, and the facts are these: On Friday morning the children of the St. Philip-street Public School, became alarmed and panic-stricken at the appearance of a gentleman, who, they said, had the appearance of a red man with protruding horns. This man had made his appearance in a very mysterious manner and frightened the children out of their wits. On the same day this representative of his Satanic majesty paid the Morris-street (colored) school a visit, and created such a consternation among the little woolly pates as has seldom been witnessed before. Wild rumors flew about the city of the presence of the Ku Klux Klan. The children shrieked in fear, and distracted parents ran about in frantic search after their children, whom they already saw kidnapped and carried off by this "all bones and bloody head." The teachers of the schools finally succeeded in calming the pupils, and the matter had nearly been forgotten, when yesterday the whole school again was thrown into a panic by a second advent of the apparition. No explanation of this mysterious affair had been made. . . . It is hoped that (the schools) will not be again be visited by this bugbear who frightens the children so badly.

Source: "Consternation among the Negro Children in Charleston," Charleston Courier, July 21, 1868. http://query.nytimes.com/gst/abstract.html?res=9900E6D9103 AEF34BC4C51DFB1668383679FDE.

3. Government Investigation

From the moment the first Klansmen donned white robes adorned with
occult symbols and rode on horseback around Pulaski, Tennessee, they have
tried to capture the imagination and attention of their fellow Americans.
They succeeded immediately through their outlandish behavior and calls to
intimidate or even destroy all whom they deemed responsible for the defeat

of the South in the Civil War and to those who worked to help blacks gain equality through education and their inclusion in the political process.

The Klan spread like wildfire throughout the South, particularly after naming Forrest as its Grand Wizard. In just a few years after its founding, Klan activity had alarmed the United States government to the point in which the Congress passed the Enforcement Acts, including the Ku Klux Klan Act of 1871, which for all intent destroyed the organization.

The Enforcement Acts were a result of widespread federal investigations into Klan activity. Among them was the Kuklux Committee, which worked in South Carolina in early 1871. The first excerpt from an article published in the New York Times *explained its findings. The following excerpt described the Enforcement Acts in greater detail.*

The Sub Ku-Klux Committee, consisting of Senator SCOTT and Representatives STEVENSON and VAN TRUMP, reached Washington today, returning from a sojourn of four weeks from various parts of South Carolina, where they have been investigating Kuklux outrages on the spots where they occurred. They first visited the capital, Columbia. More than a hundred refugees, who had fled from violence in various counties were there, but after examining witnesses for two days, the Committee determined to go closer to the scenes of alleged violence, and went to Spartanburg. They expected to stay there three or four days, but stayed eleven. When word got out through Spartanburg County that they were there, the whites and Negroes, victims of violence, came in by scores every day, from all directions. Murders and cruel whippings by the Kuklux bands had so terrified them that in many neighborhoods nearly every Negro man and Republican white man had slept in the woods for months every night. They showed scarified backs, gunshot wounds, maimed ears, and other proofs of the violence they had suffered.

In Limestone Springs township, 118 cases of whipping were proved. The Committee awoke every morning to find, in the yard by the hotel, a new crowd of victims of Kuklux, some including whites, who suffered outrages which cannot be described with decency. After being whipped, the victims, if well-known persons, were often commanded, under pain of death, to sign a card renouncing the Republican Party. In a file of the *South Carolina Spartan*, the Democratic newspaper, forty-two such cards were found recently published.

At Unionville, the Committee remained two days. Not an avowed white Republican was found in the place, though privately assured by a few that they would avow themselves if protected. The terror of the Negroes here is complete. The last election was carried by a Republican majority, but the Republican County officers received Kuklux notices, and all resigned or fled. The policy there has been more toward murder and less toward whipping. The killing of ten Negroes, taken from a jail by several hundred Kuklux, acting under military organization, was investigated. A prominent lawyer of the place, Mr. SHARD, a Democrat, on cross-examination, startled the Committee by stating that he believed almost every respectable unmarried man in the community belonged to the Kuklux and he believed a thousand Kuklux were within a days' march of that village. A Negro Methodist preacher named LOUIS THOMPSON, who had an appointment June 11 at Goshen Hill church, in Union County, received a Kuklux notice in the usual form not to preach. He preached, notwithstanding, to a very few, most of the congregation fleeing when they saw the notice. In the evening a clan of twenty mounted Kuklux came, tied him and whipped him, led him off several miles, dragging him part of the way tied to the horses, whipped him again until death, mutilated him in a way that cannot with propriety be described, hung him (and) threw the body into the Tiger River, leaving a notice forbidding any one to bury him.

Before the Committee returned, Senator SCOTT sent THOMPSON'S brother, now a refugee from Columbia, to Union County, with a letter to [go along with] a strong guard of United States Cavalry [to] bury the body, which was reported to be still lying half decomposed on the water's edge.

Two more days were spent in examining witnesses in Columbia. In returning from Spartanburg, one day was occupied in hearing the statements and general views of Gen. WADE HAMPTON and Gen. BUTLER, the Democratic candidate for Governor last fall.

The Committee then visited York County, where they remained nearly a week. They discovered in Yorkville a bitter spirit among the white citizens. At supper at the hotel on the evening of their arrival, Major JAMES BERRY threw a pitcher of milk over Hon. A.T. WALLACE, the representative of the District, and Hon. J.E. STEVENSON, of the Committee. They were just seating themselves at the table, and not a word had been spoken. MR. WALLACE jerked out a revolver and raised it to Berry—the ladies screaming—but the landlord threw himself before BERRY and Mr. STEVENSON coolly caught MR. WALLACE'S hand, and ordered the landlord to take that man out of the room. Half a dozen friends gathered around BERRY, and he went out. In the course of an hour, several citizens of prominence called to apologize in the amplest manner on behalf of BERRY, who was willing to go on his knees if required for what he alleged was an unintentional affront to MR. STEVENSON. It was subsequently ascertained that the business had been discussed by BERRY and his friends during the afternoon it was to be carried out, and that BERRY had proposed to use hot coffee, but had finally concluded on milk. The colored band serenaded the Committee later. . . . A crowd of young white men filled the porch of the hotel and were about the band frequently, cursing the Negroes and the Yankees in an insulting manner. As the band went away the crowd followed and nearly filled the sidewalk. The band and those with it (Negroes) were kept by two village policemen from the sidewalk. One Negro was thrust off by a policeman, who says the Negro resisted and struck him. The Negro and two men who were close by say the Negro struggled to get away from the grip of the policeman, who seized, cursed and struck him, but that the Negro did not strike. As he pulled away the policeman fired at the Negro, and continued firing until he had inflicted five wounds. The man was still living when the Committee left. The testimony taken showed that both the policeman and the mayor . . . were members of the Kuklux. No one was arrested.

. . . Col. MERRILL, in a command of a small force stationed [in York County], an officer of high character and great energy, laid before the Committee the details of sixty-eight cases of outrages which he had investigated, some of them most revolting and horrible. It was found impossible for the Committee to examine more than small part of the crowds of whipped, maimed or terror-stricken wretches who flocked in upon hearing of their coming. When the Committee adjourned, the building in which they had sat was filled, stairs, halls, and porches, with those waiting to be heard. The usual course pursued, on arriving at a place, was to divide the time they expected between the majority and the minority of the Committee. Judge VAN TRUMP usually called two or three of the most prominent lawyers, who each occupied several hours in setting forth the Democratic view of affairs, giving their opinions on the relations of the two races, the inefficiency and corruption of the State Government and the feeling of the white people toward the General Government. They always said they had heard of Kuklux, but never saw one. Generally, they seemed to regard them as a kind of vigilance committee or irregular local Police; did not consider them under a general organization, but simply to repress outbreaks. The majority then called for those who had seen and felt the Kuklux. The oaths, forms and proceeding in the Klan, councils and modes of operation when riding on raids, were fully developed. Scores of men, whom the proof showed to be Kuklux, were examined, all of whom, except a few, whose disclosures were full and important, denied any knowledge whatever of Kuklux. One who was shown to have been in several outrages, swore that he had never heard of the existence of Kuklux in his life. Judge VAN TRUMP subjected all the witnesses called by the majority to the most searching cross-examination.

The Kuklux Committee today adopted a resolution for the appointment of a subcommittee of three members to hear the testimony of a few witnesses on their way to Washington, when an adjournment will take place until the 20th of September.

Source: "Domestic News: Return of the Ku-Klux Committee from South Carolina," *New York Times,* July 30, 1871, 1. http://query.nytimes.com/gst/abstract.html?res=9A0CE5DE153CE63ABC4850DFB166838A669FDE.

4. A Beacon Of Light

Southern segregationists were not to be deterred by the findings of the Kuklux Committee. They responded by instituting a series of state and local laws that ensured the inequality of blacks in all aspects of society until the civil rights movement began to chip away at them more than seventy-five years later. But for a few years in the mid-1870s, blacks indeed seemed to be in control of their own destinies.

Between 1870 and 1871 Congress passed the Enforcement Acts—criminal codes that protected blacks' right to vote, hold office, serve on juries, and receive equal protection of laws. If the states failed to act, the laws allowed the federal government to intervene. The target of the acts was the Ku Klux Klan, whose members were murdering many blacks and some whites because they voted, held office, or were involved with schools.

Many states were afraid to take strong action against the Klan either because the political leaders sympathized with the Klan, were members, or because they were too weak to act. A number of Republican governors were afraid of sending black militia troops to fight the Klan for fear of triggering a race war. But once Congress passed the Enforcement Acts, the situation shifted. One of the Acts, the Ku Klux Klan Act of 1871, made private criminal acts federal crimes; consequently, President Grant decreed that "insurgents were in rebellion against the authority of the United States." He sent federal troops to restore law and order to many areas where violence was raging at its worst.

In nine counties of South Carolina, martial law was declared and Klansmen were tried before predominantly black juries. Much of the credit for prosecuting the Klan belonged to Amos Ackerman, Grant's Attorney General, who did his best to make the country aware of the extent of Klan violence. As a result of his efforts, a few hundred Klansmen were tried and sent to jail. Thousands of others fled or were let off with fines or warnings. By 1872, the Klan as an organization was broken. By the time the terror ended, thousands of blacks and hundreds of whites had been massacred or driven from their homes and communities.

Source: Richard Wormser, "Jim Crow Stories: The Enforcement Acts (1870–71)," The Rise and Fall of Jim Crow, Public Broadcasting Service. http://www.pbs.org/wnet/jimcrow/stories_events_enforce.html (accessed February 13, 2009).

5. Klan Intimidation

In historical terms, Southern blacks in the nineteenth century enjoyed a measure of freedom for only a few years. Slavery was abolished in 1865, but Klan intimidation and terror began that year and continued until the Enforcement Acts took hold in 1871. By the mid-1870s, the enactment of Jim Crow laws reversed the advancements and placed blacks back to the status of second-class citizen.

During those four years, however, Klansmen convicted of violating the Enforcement Acts through violent measures against blacks or whites trying to improve the lives of blacks were sent to jail. The following is a letter sent from a detective who interviewed Klan prisoners to the New York attorney general. It expressed prisoner claims they were hoodwinked by Klan leaders as to the organization's aims.

The truth to such assertions can only be speculative, but though the Klan was founded by six well-respected professionals and initially attracted those with similar backgrounds, it soon began to recruit the poorly educated, angry, and disaffected. Individual Ghouls whose actions Grand Wizard Forrest and the Klan hierarchy couldn't control began a spree of violence and killing that led to the demise of the organization. In turn, imprisoned Klansmen pointed their fingers elsewhere, accusing their leaders of deception in regard to the true nature of the KKK during the recruitment process.

Colonel Whitely, chief of the detective force, has addressed the following letter to Attorney General Williams, New York, August 9, 1872:

Sir—I have the honor to acknowledge the receipt of a communication from your department, under date of the 2d instant, enclosing copy of a letter from Gerritt Smith, Esq., addressed to the President, in relation to those convicts in the Albany Penitentiary who were convicted of violations of the Enforcement Acts, and requesting me to go to Albany and make thorough investigation into the conditions of these prisoners and report to the department my views as to the expediency of exercising Executive clemency in regard to any of them. In accordance to your request, I proceeded to Albany on the 7th for the purpose of fulfilling the duty assigned me as a means of conducting inquiries in a manner best adapted to arrive at all the facts in the case, and also to lead the prisoners to express themselves as freely as possible. I deemed it best to see each of the parties separately without any knowledge upon their part as to my official character or the object of my visit. In this I received the fullest aid from Mr. Lewis D. Pillsbury, headkeeper of the penitentiary, who brought each prisoner in separately with the simplest remark to each: "This gentleman desires to talk with you." The prisoners were mainly frank and communicative. Some of them are very poor, unlearned, and have left large families behind them, and while acknowledging that they were members of the various orders known under the general head of the Ku-Klux Klan and that they had been justly sentenced as such, plead extenuation that they had joined the order without full knowledge of its aims and objects and had been incited to deeds of violence by their leaders, who had managed to escape from the country, leaving them to bear the responsibility and the punishment of their misdeeds. A number of them stated that they had been compelled to join the order to save themselves and families from visits of the Klan. Others had entered under the supposition that it was a society organized for mutual protection, but learned subsequently that its real designs were the extermination of the Negro race and the driving out of such of the whites as were in favor of the political equality and social elevation of the blacks, these severally exhibited the heartiest condition for their misdeeds, stated that the order was only inimical to the best interests of society, and that the government was fully justified in breaking it up. In further extenuation of having been members of the order, they stated that the operations of the Ku-Klux Klan are wide-spread, embracing within its folds men of superior intelligence to whom they had been accustomed to look for advice and counsel, and who they did not suppose would lead them into any combination that contemplated personal violence and even murder if these were necessary for the accomplishment of its ends. They were told it was a good institution to put down meanness in the country and they accepted the statement implicitly. Upwards of forty examinations were made in the manner above mentioned, indicating neither prisoner knowing that any but himself had been called out, and none of them being aware as before observed, of my official position or the object of my visit. There was a singular unanimity in their statements, and a general expression of regret that they should have been drawn into an organization differing so entirely in the object in which they supposed it had in view when they joined it.

In reply to the general questions, what were the objects of the organization, the answer was almost invariably, when we joined the order we supposed it to be a society established for mutual protection, but after having been fully initiated we discovered it to be for a political purpose. Which purpose was embodied in an oath, in which we swore to oppose the Radical party in all its forms and prevent the Negroes from voting. It was this great deception that misled us and has brought us to our present condition. The condition manifested by many of these prisoners, the hearty abhorrence expressed by them for the acts, into the commission of which, they claim they were betrayed by unscrupulous and designing men of more enlightened minds, their general want of intelligence and their extreme poverty, all appeal strongly for mercy.

Source: Associated Press Dispatches: "All About the Ku-Klux Prisoners," Atlanta Constitution, August 15, 1872, 1. http://pqasb.pqarchiver.com/ajc_historic/access/524213762. html?dids=524213762:524213762&FMT=ABS&FMTS=ABS:AI&date=Aug+ 15%2C+1872&author=TELEGRAPH&pub=The+Atlanta+Constitution+(1869- 1875)&edition=&startpage=1&desc=All+About+the+Ku-Klux+Prisoners.

6. Thirst For Revenge

Though the second Klan era, led by William Simmons, would not be ushered in by a cross-burning ceremony on Stone Mountain on the outskirts of Atlanta for another three-and-a-half months, some claim it really began with the reaction to the murder of fourteen-year-old Mary Phagan, whose body was discovered in a Georgia pencil factory in 1915.

Anti-Semitic sentiment and a thirst for revenge immediately convinced many that the perpetrator was Jewish factory owner Leo Frank, who was soon convicted of the crime despite a compelling lack of evidence. He was found guilty and given a death sentence. But when that sentence was reduced to life imprisonment, a mob mentality took over. A group decided to avenge Phagan's murder by abducting Frank from the prison grounds and lynching him.

The elaborate nature of the scheme is noted in the following Atlanta Constitution *story published the day after Frank's murder. This sample of the article begins after members of the mob had reached the convict's room. The last excruciating moments of his life were about to begin.*

Entering the room occupied by Frank, he was awakened by a bitter exclamation from the leader. Hardly had his eyes opened when he was grabbed by the wrist, and the fingers of the second masked man sank into his hair, clutching a handful and pulling him in this manner out of bed.

Frank groaned in pain. The men snapped a pair of handcuffs upon his wrist and began making for the door. The capture was so orderly that but few prisoners—and only those adjacent to the empty bunk—were disturbed from their sleep.

When the captors had reached the entrance, Warden Smith and the superintendent still at their head, the superintendent was asked to go along with them. "I'll be damned if I go anywhere with you," he replied vehemently.

Just for this caustic retort, the lynchers permitted [the superintendent] to remain manacled while they released the wrists of the warden.

The machines stood at the curb, their engines running ready for a speedy getaway. The men who were keeping guard over the overpowered sentries stood at their post, one of them lighting a cigarette. Seven machines almost simultaneously veered into the road and shot toward Eatonton. Frank, his half-wakened mind still unable to grasp the full purport of his captivity, was stretched in the tonneau of the first machine and he mumbled incoherently.

Barely had the tall lamps of the fleeing cars merged into the darkness than the prison authorities hurried to give alarm. The telephone was their first resort. It was dead, the wires having been cut in accord with the elaborate plans of the murderous expedition.

A courier was sent to the home of Captain Jay H. Ennis, member of the legislature from Baldwin County and commandant of the Baldwin Blues, the detachment of militia in Milledgeville. Messengers were also dispatched to the homes of other officials. Within an incredibly short time, a squad of pursuers was in full flight

The telephone and telegraph wires had been severed. This had been done by the two "advance" men sent ahead of the lynchers. Because of their unfamiliarity with the telegraph and telephone systems, however, the "advance" workers had overlooked a single telegraph strand connecting Milledgeville with Augusta. Over this wire was flashed the first news of the liberation. And it was over this wire that the Constitution's information was gained shortly after midnight.

The minuteness of detail from which the tragedy was executed indicated a mastermind at lynchcraft. Foreseeing instant pursuit, a single car, loaded with at least seven or eight lynchers, was detoured in the vicinity of Eatonton, turned into the roadway that leads to the bridge spanning Little River, with instructions to decoy pursuers with gunshots.

A detached machine sped to the river bridge and there fired desultory volleys, sprinkling their shells over the ground when they had been ejected.

The oncomers heard the shots and hastened in their direction. But the fleeing machine, when its decoying mission was finished, sped up, skirted a few country byways, and rejoined the main body of lynchers. The discovery of shells, which smelled of new-burnt powder, sprinkled along the river's edge, created the report published in Atlanta Tuesday that Frank's body had been discovered at that spot.

The decoy worked splendidly. The posse was momentarily diverted. Presently, however, they renewed the trail, finding, in the dawning light, the path of chains that covered the rear tire of each of the fugitive autos. These chain tracks were followed for two miles or so when they suddenly disappeared, giving place to the tread of bare tires.

The fugitives had cunningly foreseen even this possibility, and had gone to the trouble and delay of detaching their chains so that their tire tracks might not be distinguished from those of the ordinary auto traffic.

Skirting Eatonton, and keeping to the less traveled roadways, the fleeing machines rushed onto Roswell and into the homestretch to the grove where the lynching was staged.

Frank was bound and manacled, sitting upright on the rear seat of the forward machine. In the tonneau beside him sat four men. The muzzles of rifles bristled from the car—from all, in fact. But what Frank said, or what the men who were to slay him said to him, is not known.

The lynchers' autos were seen by William Frey in the wakening sun as they sped by his house, a stone's throw from the scene of the lynching. A customarily early riser, he was standing upon his porch as the line of machines swept by.

Oddly enough—perhaps by intuition, more than anything else, he, like all other natives of Cobb County, having heard, read, and seen so much of the Frank case—he recognized the features of the famous prisoner sitting in the tonneau, clad in his prison night shirt. "Well, I guess it won't be long until Mary Phagan's vindicated," he remarked to the household as he reentered the doorway to get his hat and travel up the road. "I saw 'em hauling Frank up the road just now," he added, donning his hat, departed up the road, trudging in his dust, eyes directed along the wayside for signs of the lynchers.

He was one of the first to reach the scene. The lynchers had deserted their spot. It was in the woodland thicket across the road from the cottage in which Mary Phagan once lived with her parents. The trees composing the grove are huge oaks covered with heavy foliage.

Frank's body swung in the slight breeze from the limb of a hollow oak in the heart of the thicket. Directly beneath his swaying feet ran a curving footpath, which led to a group of benches on the inside fringe of the grove. The body wore only a nightshirt made of the plain, homespun cloth of prison garb, the only distinctive mark being lettering "LMF" crocheted upon the left breast over the heart by the fingers of his wife. A trickle of blood had run from the gaping wound in the throat—inflicted by William Green a month ago in his murderous prison assault—down to the embroidered initials, and there had stopped, absorbed in the tiny mountains of cotton thread. The slayers had fashioned a robe of crocus sack to cover the lower portions of the swinging body.

That Frank was alive at the time he was strung up is undisputed. His body was warm, and there was still a faint throb of pulse when it was first discovered.

His feet were bound with bundling cord, and a pair of new steel cuffs gripped his wrists. The noose around his throat was after the design of the professional hangman. It ran from the circle of hemp around the throat up underneath the chin, and, as in legal hangings, threw the head far back around the shoulders.

The lynchers had fitted a handkerchief around Frank's eyes and tied it at the back like a blindfold.

He was strangled to death. Slowly drawn from the ground, he undoubtedly flayed the air in the death agonies of strangulation, instead of the instantaneous death by disjointment of the neck, created by the customary "drop" through the gallows.

Then, as silently as they had come, the lynchers stole away.

Source: "Mob's Own Story in Detail: How Plans Were Formed and Put into Execution Without Slightest Hitch." Atlanta Constitution, August 18, 1915, 1. http://pqasb.pqarchiver.com/ajc_historic/access/553269252.html?dids=553269252: 553269252&FMT=ABS&FMTS=ABS:AI&date=Aug+18%2C+1915&author=&pub=The+Atlanta&edition=&startpage=1&desc=MOB%27S+OWN+STORY+IN+DETAIL.

7. Movie Review For The Ages

A mere two days after William Simmons gained a charter for the Ku Klux Klan, thus launching what would become easily the most successful era in the history of the organization, a film depicting Klansmen as heroes and blacks as little more than savages reached the Atlanta theaters. The result of the overwhelming reaction to Birth of a Nation *was free and positive publicity for the reborn Klan, the extent of which a gleeful Simmons couldn't have imagined in his wildest dreams.*

Simmons already realized that the movie, which represented a giant leap forward in the art of cinematography, would be a boon to his new venture. It had been shown with great appreciation in other cities, including New York and Los Angeles. But little could anyone have anticipated the unbridled enthusiasm it received from the Atlanta audience.

That the patrons were on the edge of their seats for a thrilling conclusion could not have disturbed anyone. But that the Klansmen were portrayed literally as heroic white knights and blacks characterized as being driven by their lust of white women angered millions of more enlightened Americans, including those representing organizations such as the National Association for the Advancement of Colored People (NAACP), which had been formed just six years earlier.

A strong appreciation of the dramatics as well as the mood of the crowd was captured in this review of the movie published in the Atlanta Constitution.

. . . Griffith awakens the memories of childhood; warms the heart with romance; quickens the pulse with patriotism; forces the exultant cheer from the lips of the midst of great battles; turns the heart sick with scenes of bloodshed; dims the eyes with tears of woman's sufferings; relieves the tension of emotions with a timely humorous incident; makes you tremble for the peril of the mother passing through the lines to reach a wounded son; interests you with a faithful reproduction of Ford's Theater and the assassination of Lincoln—and when Griffith has done all these things he has just begun!

You are ushered into the ante-chamber in Washington, where a misguided man is plotting a black regime among white people—where a Mulatto woman dreams of empire. You live through a period of ruin and destruction in the country where you were born. You see the plot executed and that same country humiliated and crushed under a black heel. Former happiness is shattered by the arrogance of ignorance. You sicken at the sight of the attempt to enforce martial racial equality. Again and again the unbearable hideousness of the days of reconstruction is borne in upon you. History repeats itself upon the screen with a realism that is maddening. You could shriek for a depiction of relief and—yes, retribution. Thus, over and over, does the picture grind and pound and pulverize your emotions.

But the end is not yet.

The insufferable reasons for the Ku Klux Klan next, with a wealth of detail, an intimate knowledge that is astonishing Griffith brings a spectral army into being before your eyes.

Omit these details of dangerous and mysterious night meetings of men, and of the perils of women secretly making strange white garments with crosses emblazoned upon them.

Comes then an appointed night when two men—men on horses garbed in white from head to hoof—ride out from behind an ordinary country barn that you have seen a hundred times, and canter off down the road. At the top of a hill, they stop. One holds high a cross of fire. Upon a distant hill other figures catch the signal. Now a group of white-clad horsemen has foregathered. The scene shifts to a great open field at night. There is a blood-curdling trumpet blast from the orchestra pit pitched in a minor key. A troop of white figures upon spirited horses dashes at breakneck speed into the picture and wheels into position. There is a cheer from the audience. Comes another blood-curdling trumpet call and another troop, and then another and another and another. Men grimly determine upon a last desperate chance to rescue women and homes and civilization from an unspeakable curse are gathering for the work at hand. At last as far as the camera's scope can gather is assembled a vast, grim host in white. One more troop—they are a little late; you think they have come a long distance—wheels into place, right in the camera's very eye!

"The Little Colonel," hero of the story, and such a hero!—takes his place at the head of the white multitude. Again the trumpet blast. "The Little Colonel" rises in his stirrups and holds aloft a cross of fire. The host moves forward.

The awful restraint of the audience is thrown to the winds. Many rise from their seats. With the roar of thunder a shout goes up. Freedom is here. Justice is at hand! Retribution has arrived!

Source: Ned McIntosh, "Birth of a Nation Thrills Tremendous Atlanta Audience," Atlanta Constitution, December 7, 1915, 7. http://pqasb.pqarchiver.com/ajc_historic/access/553455892.html?dids=553455892:553455892&FMT=ABS&FMTS=ABS:AI&date=Dec+7%2C+1915&author=Ned+McIntosh&pub=The+Atlanta+Constitution+(1881-2001)&edition=&startpage=7&desc=%22Birth+of+a+Nation%22+Thrills+Tremendous+Atlanta+Audience.

8. Last Gasp For Second Klan

That the tolerance and even embracing of the Klan over the years has proven far stronger in the South than in other areas of the country is an accepted fact. And the same holds true for the organization's relationship with the media. Even when the entire nation had been turned off by Klan violence in the 1950s and 1960s, much of the Southern media walked hand-in-hand with the Klan or at least attempted to justify many of its actions.

One example of the differences in media perception of the Klan was its coverage of the August 1925 march in Washington. As one can gather from the following excerpts, the event was glorified by the Atlanta Constitution, *but downplayed and even ridiculed to an extent by* Time Magazine.

Klan Imperial Wizard Hiram Wesley had claimed that up to 200,000 Klansmen from throughout the country would be attending. But as the march drew near, he drastically reduced the prediction. Local Klan leaders in states near the nation's capital scrambled to lure its members to the march, which resulted in the participation of several thousand Klansman representing Pennsylvania. There were virtually none, however, from such KKK strongholds as Georgia, Louisiana, South Carolina, Alabama, Tennessee, Mississippi, and Texas, a fact that the Constitution *failed to mention, but was included in a much shorter* Time *story.*

The Klan was in the process of losing millions of members at the time of the event. The scandal involving Indiana Klan leader David Curtis Stephenson, as well as media reports of Klan violence in other areas of the country, had convinced most of its members to resign. From reading the Constitution's *coverage of the march on Washington, one might believe the newspaper was attempting to revitalize the image of the organization. One might also gather that the fact that* Time *used fewer than five hundred words to describe the march indicated a belief by its editors that Klan influence had greatly waned.*

The following excerpt from the Constitution *uses flowery language and a positive tone. But note the sarcasm in the* Time *excerpt, as well as the forwarding of the notion that the event was a disappointment.*

In a great white flood of humanity, liberally speckled with American flags, the Ku Klux Klan poured its strength from the capital down Pennsylvania Avenue Saturday, marching to a great open field underneath the tower of the Washington Monument, where a weird night spectacle was staged.

. . . From beginning to end of the demonstration, not the slightest disorder was reported to the police. Although the District of Columbia National Guard had been summoned to its armory for drills, there was no suggestion that it would be called into service to maintain order. The citizen soldiers went through routine work only.

The streets of the capital were packed along the line of march as the Klansmen paraded slowly by, in their long white robes and white peaked caps, but unmasked, and smiling genially at their cordial welcome.

The procession lacked the military precision of other parades which have marched down the historic avenue in the past. Those near the numerous hands in the line of march quickened their pace to a semi-military pace, but for the most part, the marchers shuffled along informally. They all seemed to enjoy the curiosity they had aroused. They strung out across the street thirty-two abreast.

There was much applause and hand clapping from the huge crowd, which lined the avenue and hung out of the windows of buildings all over the route. Everyone appeared to be in high good humor.

Excerpt from a speech delivered after the march by Rev. A. H. Gulledge, Minister of the Church of Christ in Columbus, Ohio:

"There can be peace and love in the world and this country only so long as every race and color keeps the place that God gave it, without trying to lap over to the country of white Protestants or to intermarry with the white race."

Source: Thomas L. Stokes, "Thousands March in Klan Parade through Capital," Atlanta Constitution, August 9, 1925, 1. http://pqasb.pqarchiver.com/ajc_historic/access/562841802.html?dids=562841802:562841802&FMT=ABS&FMTS=ABS:AI&date=Aug+9%2C+1925&author=THOMAS+L+STOKES&pub=The+Atlanta+Constitution+(1881-2001)&edition=&startpage=1&desc=THOUSANDS+MARCH+IN+KLAN%27S+PARADE+THROUGH+CAPITAL.

From 3:00 to 7:00 through the heat the multitude gathered into the sylvan theatres near the Washington Monument; the great drought within them was mocked by a downpour of rain. A prayer, a speech or two, and the pounding, pounding rain brought the meeting to a close.

Source: "Procession," *Time* magazine 6, no. 7 (August 17, 1925).

9. The Attack On Marge Oberholtzer

No single incident doomed the second era of the Klan with greater assured-ness than the vicious attack perpetrated by Indiana Grand Dragon David Curtis Stephenson on female acquaintance Madge Oberholtzer.

In a mere ten years, the Klan had built itself up from nothing to a major social and political force in America with more than 4 million members. It had done so by curbing its reputation for violence, at least publicly, and the championing of family values and civic responsibility. The Klan also backed Prohibition, which was the law of the land at the time. So when Stephenson was found to have brutally beaten Oberholtzer in a drunken fury, the huge majority of Klan members and the rest of the American public deemed it a slap in the face to all the organization claimed to stand for. Though other reports of Klan violence played a role in a mass defection, the Stephenson case did more to reduce membership from more than 4 million to 45,000 in a span of five years than any other factor.

The brutality of Stephenson's attack on Oberholtzer, who felt so ashamed by the incident that she later committed suicide by taking poison, was revealed in the court proceedings, which resulted in a twenty-year prison sentence for the defendant. Stephenson's bodyguards, Earl Gentry and Earl Klenck, also went on trial, but were acquitted.

Stephenson was initially convicted of second-degree murder by the jury, which would have given him a jail term of twenty-five years. But the jury reconsidered two days later and increased the charge to first-degree murder, which resulted in life imprisonment. Stephenson was paroled in 1950, but violated the parole by disappearing for three months and was then captured in Minneapolis. He was paroled again in 1956 on the con-dition that he never return to Indiana. Five years later, he was arrested for allegedly trying to sexually assault a sixteen-year-old girl, but was released after paying a $300 fine. He died in Johnson City, Tennessee, in 1966.

The following excerpt of an article reporting on Stephenson's murder trial describes the prosecutor's closing arguments.

"Excoriated yesterday in the State's closing arguments, the three defendants were assailed with new fury today by Ralph Kane, who spoke for the prosecution for more than two hours, and closed sixteen hours of argument. He called Stephenson a "hideous monster" and a "serpent who should be put away for the protection of the daughters of his future."

The three defendants sat unmoved during the verbal lashing.

"These men are criminals," declared the prosecutor. "By their acts they drove that girl to the position that she believed life held nothing for her but shame, and she took poison. They are as guilty of murder as though they had stabbed her in the heart."

Source: Associated Press, "Finds Ex-Klan Head Murdered Woman," *New York Times*, November 15, 1925, 1.

10. Comeuppance For The Klan

Angered by media reports of Klan violence in the mid-1920s that proved damaging to the organization, Imperial Wizard Hiram Wesley Evans overstepped his bounds in 1927. With Klan membership in the process of falling a mind-boggling 99 percent from 1924 to 1930, Evans took action when a group of rebellious Pennsylvania Klansmen broke away from the Invisible Empire. He filed a $100,000 lawsuit against them in an attempt to force them back in.

The result was a disaster for Evans. Little did he suspect that the Pennsylvania Klansmen would react by battling back in court and alleging that the Imperial Wizard had involved the organization in a number of violent and illegal acts. A string of witnesses took the stand to tell of grisly stories of Klan activities backed by Evans ranging from intimidation to murder. Newspapers throughout the country picked up on the court case and the witness accounts. The disgusted and angry judge threw out Evans' case.

Among those who entered depositions in the case against Evans were former Imperial Wizard Simmons, who was still seething from his ouster from that position three years earlier, and Stephenson, who was in jail following his attack on Oberholtzer. Simmons claimed that the sprees of violence alleged in court were never a part of Klan activity when he had been Imperial Wizard. But it was Stephenson's deposition that proved most damaging, as the following excerpt from a 1928 article in the Literary Digest *indicates.*

One piece of anti-Klan testimony which aroused much newspaper attention was a deposition made by D.C. Stephenson, now in the Indiana State prison under conviction of murder. Stephenson had been hired in the counsels of the Klan, and gave a detailed account of how Hiram Wesley Evans maneuvered six years ago to make himself successor as supreme head or Imperial Wizard of the Klan to its modern founder William J. Simmons. The full story runs through more than 40,000 words and, according to the *New York Evening World* "is the most astonishing record of the use of criminal means, including debauchery, blasting of reputations, torture, and even murder, for the purpose of obtaining and retaining control of a secret organization of intimidation that has been revealed since the exposure of the activities of the Molly McGuires in the Pennsylvania coal-fields half a century ago." Only a part of this deposition was admitted into evidence, the chief items, according to a *New York World* dispatch, were

His charge that Grand Dragons were instructed by Evans to follow his order blindly, and that if they failed to do so they would be unseated, punished, and their characters attacked.

His allegation that the "black-masked robed gang" was authorized by Evans and was the official robe when Klansmen went on killing and whipping parties.

His charge that Evans had boasted that a Negro had been burned at the stake in Texas; that Klansmen had caught off the Negro's ears; and that "KKK" had been branded on the forehead of another Negro.

His testimony that after a riot in Perth Amboy, New Jersey, in 1923, Evans had told him "if the Klan can make it look as if we are being persecuted, it will help increase our membership."

Source: "A Judicial Spanking for the Klan," Literary Digest, April 28, 1928. Old-MagazineArticles.com. http://www.oldmagazinearticles.com/pdf/KKK_in_court-1928.pdf (accessed February 17, 2009).

11. Going Undercover

Among the most fascinating people to ever don a white mask and robe was a Klansman who wasn't really a Klansman at all.

His name was Stetson Kennedy. Working underground for the Non-Sectarian Anti-Nazi League, Kennedy infiltrated the Klan after World War II and wrote a book about his experiences titled I Rode with the Ku Klux Klan, *which was later reissued as* The Klan Unmasked. *He gained first-hand knowledge in Klan terror and was forced to bite his tongue and hide his anger when confronted with the most brutal beatings and even murders of Southern blacks.*

Kennedy supplied inside information to the likes of media giants such as Drew Pearson and Walter Winchell. Most interesting was that he also provided secret Klan codes to the producers of the Superman *radio program. Superman would then set off to defeat Klansmen, who were shouting secret passwords throughout those particular episodes. Real-life Klansmen grew frustrated at having fictional Klansmen giving away inside information while being destroyed by a popular superhero whose show was being enjoyed by millions of Americans.*

Little did Klan leaders know that it was Kennedy who motivated Pearson to demand an opportunity to broadcast from the hallowed Invisible Empire's Stone Mountain site in 1946. The Klan closed it down temporarily, which forced Pearson to speak on the steps of the state capitol building in Atlanta and reveal that the Klan planned on having an Atlanta Cyclops appointed as the head of the Georgia Bureau of Investigation, which would have allowed Klan violence to continue unabated. Pearson also regularly read the minutes of Klan meetings on the air.

Kennedy eventually started a campaign called "Frown Power" in which he simply urged people to frown when listening to anyone espousing bigotry publicly or privately.

One of the most disturbing passages of The Klan Unmasked *told of his experience with a group of Klansmen (who called themselves Klavaliers) bent on killing a black man for allegedly trying to pick up a white woman. They shoved victim James Martin into a car, drove just outside the county line, and pushed him out of the car. That's when the Klansmen sprung into action.*

Almost before I knew what was happening, both carloads of Klavaliers had swarmed around him, and were kicking at his prostrated form amid a torrent of profanity. The Negro groaned and doubled over to protect his groin, but he made no plea for mercy. I felt like vomiting, and was glad my face was masked to hide my disgust. With great effort I kicked in the direction of the Negro, missing deliberately. Randal, meanwhile, was standing on the sidelines, calmly putting on his robe. That done, he stepped up, and the kicking subsided.

"You'd better say your prayers, nigger!" he said. "Your time has come."

"I don't know why y'all treating me like this," he groaned.

"You know better than to pick up a white woman!" Randal said. "And now you're going to pay the penalty."

After beating Martin further, the Klansmen began firing shots at his feet, demanding that he dance. He was then told to run down the road, but warned to remain on the road. Martin might have figured he had been spared, but he would have figured wrong.

Randal climbed back into the cab and motioned for us to get in. The Negro started on a slow, painful lope down the road, and Randal began to follow. Leaning out of the window, he fired at the Negro's heels.

"Step on it!" he yelled, increasing the speed of the car. Slim and the others followed suit, leaning out of the windows, firing and cursing. We kept going faster and faster, and the distance between the cab and the fleeing form grew perilously shorter. The Negro had been running in the center of the road, between the ruts, when suddenly he started to cross the road and head for the woods. He stumbled in the rut and fell. Randal jammed on the brakes, but there was a sickening thud, and the car passed over the Negro's body. I turned away, sick. Without looking, I knew he was dead.

As was the custom at the time, the local newspaper ran a one-inch notice on the back page the following morning stating that a Negro cab driver had been the apparent victim of a hit-and-run accident.

Source: Stetson Kennedy, *The Klan Unmasked* (Boca Raton, Fla.: Florida Atlantic University Press, 1990), 109–111.

12. Backlash In The South

The notion that the majority or even a large percentage of Southern whites ever fully embraced the Ku Klux Klan is ungrounded. Equally untrue is the belief that the law in the majority of the South worked hand-in-hand with the Klan, giving them free rein to terrorize blacks. And one who believes that all blacks were left cowering by the threat of Klan violence, at least before the civil rights movement, would also be mistaken. There was a huge discrepancy between the number of Southern citizens and police officers that believed in the righteousness of a segregated society and those who actively backed and sympathized with Klan activity.

Klan support in the South grew with the threat of integration in the late 1950s and early 1960s. But in the years immediately following World War II, the organization simply didn't boast much influence, even in the Deep South. Many state leaders called for new laws, such as those disallowing Klansmen to wear their regalia in public, thereby stripping them of much of their power. Others simply didn't want to rock the boat. They felt that Klan action against blacks brought attention to the segregated South and its injustices and hastened calls for integration.

In the book, Hooded Americanism, *David M. Chalmers wrote about the post-war era and the pervasive anti-Klan sentiment in the South.*

Two particular characteristics of the postwar Klan emerged clearly. The first was the open pattern of resistance in numerous communities where the Klan was active. The second was that while the Klan could still commit violence and inspire terror, the organization itself gained little prestige. Jeers and laughter, from Negro as well as white, greeted many a Klan speech, parade, and cross burning. In Greenville, Georgia, Negroes lined the road for a Klan parade; giggling children drumming on kitchen pots and pans followed the marchers and an old woman called out to Klansmen, "Send us your sheets, white folks, we'll wash 'em." When the Grand Dragon, Samuel Green himself, spoke in Columbia, South Carolina, white students from the university heckled him and tossed stink bombs. In Talladega, Alabama, a twelve-year-old boy kicked down a blazing Klan cross and an armed group of men went out in search of Klansmen. During the summer of 1950, students at all-Negro Atlanta University were asked to answer a detailed questionnaire about violence and security in their communities. Half of those questioned said the Klan was operating in their areas, although more than two thirds of those living in rural districts and small towns reported no. The city police were believed to be increasingly, though not generously, likely

A fiery cross burned by Ku Klux Klan members at a meeting in Florida, 1950. Some of the Klan members lowered their masks while pictures were being taken. Source: *AP Photo/stf.*

to take action against the Klan, as were responsible members of the Negro and white communities. Fifty per cent of those from rural areas indicated that the Klan was feared, but more than two thirds of the small-town and city dwellers said it was not. [Mississippi newspaper editor] Hodding Carter commented in 1949 that while the Klan of the 1920s had been politically powerful and an overawing organization in the 1920s, the South was not willing to permit that to happen again.

Source: David Chalmers, *Hooded Americanism* (Durham, N.C.: Duke University Press, 1987), 334.

13. No Freedom For Freedom Riders

The morality of the civil rights movement and even the Northerners who traveled to the South to further the cause is rarely questioned. The Freedom Riders who were beaten up by Klansman and other racists as they sought to integrate public places in the Deep South are generally considered righteous and brave in today's society. But the majority of Americans polled in the early 1960s expressed their belief that the Northern civil rights activists should have been minding their own business. The opinions were gathered after many of those Freedom Riders had been brutalized.

The national media was no different. Note in the third paragraph of this Time Magazine *excerpt the opinion that the Congress of Racial Equality (CORE) was out to provoke trouble. Though the reporting was otherwise sympathetic to the cause of the Freedom Riders, the article mirrored the views of many Americans who felt that the group should have expected the violent reaction they received.*

On a bus traveling through the Deep South, a youthful Negro said calmly: "We can take anything the white man can dish out, but we want our rights. We know what they are—and we want them now."

The young Negro [was one of the] central figures last week in a national drama. It was a drama of conflict and violence. It saw U.S. marshals and martial law in Alabama. It saw cops with police dogs on patrol in Mississippi. It was the drama of the Freedom Riders, and it represented a new and massive assault against segregation in the U.S. South.

The assault was launched late last month when a band of six whites and seven Negroes set out to ride by bus from Washington to New Orleans. The integrated trip was sponsored by the Congress of Racial Equality, a Manhattan-based organization. Its purpose was to prove, by provoking trouble, that Southern interstate travel is still segregated in fact, although integrated by law. The original Freedom Riders passed with little incident through Virginia, North Carolina, South Carolina, and Georgia. They then came to Alabama—where they found the trouble they wanted.

For that, they could in part thank Alabama Governor John Patterson. A militant segregationist who solicited Ku Klux Klan support in his election campaign, Patterson once said that integration would come to Alabama only "over my dead body." In his inaugural address Patterson declared: "I will oppose with every ounce of energy I possess and will use every power at my command to prevent any mixing of white and Negro races in the classrooms of this state." Said he as the Freedom Riders approached: "The people of Alabama are so enraged that I cannot guarantee protection for this bunch of rabble-rousers."

Source: "Crisis in Civil Rights," *Time* magazine 77, no. 23 (June 2, 1961): 14–18.

14. A Southern Pastor's View

Arguably the most publicized Klan crime during the civil rights movement occurred on June 21, 1964. On that date, an elaborate plot concocted by Klansmen including the sheriff and deputy of Neshoba County in Mississippi resulted in the murder of civil rights workers Michael Schwerner, Andrew Goodman, and James Chaney.

Federal authorities searched for their bodies for several months before finding them in an earthen dam near the small Mississippi town of Philadelphia. During that search, many Philadelphians offered their opinions that the Klan targeted Schwerner because he had been working in the area for several months, wore a beatnik-style beard, and looked particularly Jewish. They believed Klansman angered by the intervention of Northern civil rights workers into what they perceived as the affairs of Southerners decided to make an example of Schwerner.

It took some bravery to speak out against the Klan, but that's what Philadelphia First Methodist Church pastor Clay Lee did after the bodies of the civil rights workers were uncovered. The following excerpt from an article published shortly thereafter quotes Lee, who spoke openly about the situation.

Even today there are Philadelphians who say they cannot comprehend "all this fuss over two Jews and a nigger."

But at last, a few Philadelphians are beginning to break silence and comment openly on the undercurrents of fear and guilt.

"People will tell you everything is rosy here," said the Rev. Clay Lee, pastor of the First Methodist Church, but that's a lot of hogwash. I've been a minister 15 years in Mississippi and I've never seen so much tension."

"What bothers me most," he said, "is the unwillingness of so many people to face the fact that this was a premeditated murder. I honestly don't know one member of the Klan. But beyond the shadow of a doubt they are here and they were mixed up in this."

" . . . So many people are hollering 'you gotta stick together,'" he said. "But I'm a little careful what I stick together for and stick with."

Source: Homer Bigart, "Wide Klan Plot Is Hinted in One of 3 Rights Killings," *New York Times,* November 29, 1964, 1.

15. Two Who Changed

While hard-core Klansmen were bombing churches and murdering civil rights workers in the mid–1960s, a more intellectual brand of racism continued in the Deep South. The fervent belief in white superiority was not limited to Klansmen. Others also felt that blacks were simply incapable of drastically raising their status, which rendered integration and equality an impossibility.

The three articles excerpted below capture the ability of both learned and uneducated racists to soften with the times and change their views about race relations. The first was an editorial written in 1965 by Dr. Clayton Sullivan, a Baptist preacher in Tylertown, a tiny village in southwestern Mississippi. Sullivan appeared to be among those who doubted black potential despite his understanding that the Jim Crow laws and embedded racism played a role in the social and behavioral gaps he wrote about in the following controversial article that appeared in the Saturday Evening Post. *The second was from a foreword of a book,* Called to Preach, Condemned to Survive: The Education of Clayton Sullivan, *written twenty years later about Sullivan's change of heart. The third is about Elwin Wilson, a violent Klansman in the 1960s who forty-eight years later received media attention when he begged for forgiveness from a man he had brutally beaten in 1961.*

Sullivan, who had earned his doctorate from Southern Baptist Theological Seminary and had studied at the Harvard Divinity School, expressed opinions about perceived differences between blacks and whites encompassing behavioral and moral issues also held by Klansmen and other staunch segregationists. He believed that white Northerners and liberals didn't understand that white Southerners were fighting against integration because they simply didn't want to be exposed to what they considered to be an unsavory race of people. Others argued that it was the white South that prevented blacks from gaining the education and social opportunities to advance in those areas. And though Sullivan touched on the possibility that blacks could improve their lot, he argued that immediate integration would prove disastrous.

His views changed dramatically as time marched on and integration took root in the South. In 2001, he wrote the book, Jesus and the Sweet Pilgrim Baptist Church: A Fable, *which was lauded by black Academy Award winner Morgan Freeman. The book, which was about Jesus returning to earth as a Jewish woman who visits a black church, expressed Sullivan's yearning for continued improvement in race relations in the South. But he seemed quite doubtful of that possibility when he penned the controversial editorial in the* Saturday Evening Post. *The following excerpt expresses those doubts, as well as his perceptions of the moral and behavioral difference between rural blacks and whites:*

The gap can be seen only too clearly in the aspect that is the least "nice" of all. By and large many of the rural Negroes in the South have not learned even elementary hygiene. If this sounds like a trivial complaint, then try to envision the realities we face. I wonder if it has ever dawned upon critics of the South that one of the reasons Southerners find the idea of integration so abhorrent is because of the Negro's physical uncleanliness? Doctors have discussed with me the difficulties they have in dealing with Negroes who come to them for medical help. Dirt and filth, giving off an emetic stench, often is caked on the patients' bodies. There are dentists in my acquaintance who have told me of Negroes with tartar caked so thickly that it is literally impossible to see their teeth.

"This condition is related to the primitive living conditions of rural Negroes. One of the doctors in my congregation remarked to me, "All too many of our Negroes live like swine in pigpens." The doctor's observation, though unpleasant, is true. With my own eyes I have seen Negro houses in which Negroes defecate through crude holes in the floor. I have seen Negro homes where windows are used as convenient latrines. With my own eyes I have seen Negroes to whom knives, forks and spoons are as unknown as linen napkins. That many Negroes live like swine in pigpens may not be just or Christian, but it is a social reality. White Southerners do not relish the idea of instantaneous integration with people who live under such primitive conditions as these."

Source: Dr. Clayton Sullivan, "Integration Could Destroy Rural Mississippi," *Saturday Evening Post* 238, no. 7 (April 10, 1965): 10–15.

It was a fearful thing for a white Mississippian, in those terrible years, to appear to support the black demand for freedom and respect. As Clayton Sullivan tells us, it was an especially traumatic time to be a Christian minister in Mississippi's white churches. A healing word would be greeted with scorn, a prophetic word with fire. White

Mississippians found themselves isolated, angry, and bewildered—on a collision course with history. They told story after obscene story in which their hero, Governor Ross Barnett, made John F. Kennedy and Martin Luther King seem foolish and contemptible. To most of the rest of the nation it was Ross Barnett and his loyal followers who seemed foolish and contemptible, even criminal. In their pathetic attempts to ridicule their enemies white Mississippians continued to delude themselves, even when it was clear that they would not win, things would never again be the way they had been for a hundred years. But white Mississippians wanted to believe they would win. Their rage and contempt would issue first in filthy stories and then in the shedding of blood. But their enemies kept coming—the black students and the Northern white preachers and the federal marshals and the civil rights lawyers—and they could not kill them all. And in the end, Clayton Sullivan rightly says, "The Negro's liberation from raw racism has delivered Southern whites from raw racism also."

Source: Don Haymes, Editor-in-chief, Foreword to *Called to Preach, Condemned to Survive: The Education of Clayton Sullivan* (Macon, Ga.: Mercer University Press, 1986), xi–xii.

Elwin Wilson was an unabashed racist, the sort who once hung a black doll from a noose outside his home. John Lewis was a young civil rights leader bent on changing laws, if not hearts and minds, even if it cost him his life.

They faced each other at a South Carolina bus station during a protest in 1961. Wilson joined a white gang that jeered Lewis, attacked him, and left him bloodied on the ground.

Forty-eight years later, the men met again—this time so Wilson could apologize to Lewis and express regret for his hatred. Lewis, now a congressman from Atlanta, greeted his former tormentor at his Capitol Hill office.

"I just told him that I was sorry," Wilson, 72, said in a telephone interview Wednesday as he traveled home to Rock Hill, South Carolina. For years, he said, he tried to block the incident out of his mind "and couldn't do it."

Lewis said Wilson is the first person involved in the dozens of attacks against him during the civil rights era to step forward and apologize. When they met Tuesday, Lewis offered forgiveness without hesitation.

"I was very moved," said Lewis. "He was very, very sincere, and I think it takes a lot of raw courage to be willing to come forward the way he did. . . . I think it will lead to a great deal of healing."

Wilson said he had felt an urge to voice his remorse for years. He talked about his past activities a few weeks ago with a friend, and the friend asked him where he thought he might go if he died.

"I said probably hell," Wilson said. "He said, 'Well, you don't have to.'"

Source: Ben Evans, Associated Press, "Man Who Beat Civil Rights Leader Asks Forgiveness." MSNBC online, February 5, 2009. http://www.msnbc.msn.com/id/29025477/ (accessed February 13, 2009).

16. A Sham Murder Trial

Trials of Klansmen accused of murdering blacks or civil rights workers in the South during the Jim Crow era were considered mostly shams. All-white juries generally acquitted the accused even in the face of overwhelming evidence.

One such case in Alabama occurred in May 1965, when twenty-one-year-old Klansman Collie Leroy Wilkins was one of three charged with the murder of Detroit housewife Viola Liuzzo, who had traveled to Selma to participate in a civil rights march (the other two were scheduled to stand trial that fall). The trial featured testimony from black man Leroy Moton, who was in the passenger seat when Liuzzo, the driver of the vehicle on a highway near Selma, was shot and killed. Also testifying for the prosecution was FBI informant Gary Thomas Rowe, who rode in the car with the Klansmen and witnessed the murder.

The dramatics of defense attorney Matt H. Murphy, Jr., stole the show. A Klansman himself, Murphy excoriated Rowe and Liuzzo in his summation. He spoke about Rowe first before moving quickly on to Liuzzo.

Murphy's ranting swayed at least two members of the jury. The ten to two vote for conviction resulted in a mistrial and three days later the three accused killers were celebrated in a Klan parade. Murphy was killed in a car accident three months later, which prompted former Birmingham

*mayor and staunch segregationist Art Hanes to assume the duties of defense
attorney. An all-white jury acquitted the three defendants on October 20,
which led once again to federal prosecution. And on December 3, 1965, all
three defendants were found guilty and sentenced to ten years in jail.*

The following is an excerpt of a Time Magazine *article describing
Murphy's appeal to the jury.*

"You know [Rowe is] a liar and a perjurer, holding himself out to
be a white man, and worse than a white nigger!"

"And here's another strange thing. This white woman [Liuzzo].
White woman?" He paused, then asked, "Where is that N.A.A.C.P.
card?" He held up an N.A.A.C.P. membership card that was among
Mrs. Liuzzo's effects.

"I'm proud of my heritage. I'm proud to be a white man. And I'm
proud that I stand upon my feet and I stand for white supremacy. Not
black supremacy, not the mixing and mongrelizing of the races, not
the biggest onslaughts of the civil rights movement that has invaded
your quiet little county, the Martin Luther Kings . . . the white Zionists that run that organization. The Zionists that run that bunch of
niggers. And when white people join up to 'em, they become white
niggers."

". . . Mrs. Liuzzo," he cried, "was up there singin' 'we shall overcome, we will overcome, we will overcome.' What in God's name
were they tryin' to overcome? To overcome God himself? And do
unto the white people what God said you shall not do because there'll
be thorns in your eyes, thorns in your flesh; if you intermarry with a
servile race, then you shall be destroyed!!"

Source: "The Trial," *Time* magazine 85, no. 20 (May 14, 1965): 27–29.

17. Words From Robb

*Though the prevailing thought is that the conservative, intellectual
approach to promoting the Klan died when David Duke left the organization, those who understand Thomas Robb might think differently. As of
this writing, Robb is the national director of the Knights of the Ku Klux
Klan. And like the former Knights leader, Robb has softened the traditional Klan rhetoric about white supremacy, espousing instead white pride
and the categorizing of black-on-white crime as a hate crime.*

Robb's argument has been prevalent among Klan leaders since organizations such as the Southern Poverty Law Center and the Anti-Defamation League began tracking Klan violence against minorities and taking the perpetrators to court. But Robb, whose organization has been battling painfully low membership numbers since the turn of the century, hoped to latch on to issues about which a higher percentage of Americans feel strongly. He has railed against corporations taking jobs out of the country to save vast amounts of money in operating their businesses. Such a view has been embraced by millions of liberals and conservatives alike.

Robb, a member of the John Birch Society in high school who later earned a Doctor of Theology degree from the Rocky Mountain Kingdom Bible Institute, earned notoriety when he organized a protest in Pulaski, Tennessee, against the Martin Luther King holiday. Six years later, he was the subject of a Time Magazine *article that tracked his transformation from a virulent, violent racist and anti-Semite to a more intellectual and passive one. The excerpt begins with a quote from Robb about blacks in America during his interview with the author.*

"This is going to sound awful crude to say this, and maybe it will come out wrong," says Robb, "but at least during the time of slavery, they earned their keep. What benefit are they to us today, after food stamps and public housing and heating their homes and caring for their children and taking them to the hospital and all the things that are done? Where's the appreciation for that, and what is the benefit to us?"

These ideas are mild compared with those Robb expressed in the past. Before remaking his image, he castigated blacks and Jews, embraced Hitler and endorsed killing homosexuals. . . . His newspapers [the *Torch* and *White Patriot*] have featured racial slurs including a cartoon showing a hanging of a black man and a bigoted ditty, the Negro National Anthem. Despite his toned-down persona, he still hawks copies of *Mein Kampf* and swears the Holocaust is a hoax.

. . . Robb's ultimate goal is to hang a WHITES ONLY sign at America's borders. He fears his race will soon disappear beneath a tide of nonwhite immigrants and homegrown minorities. It is his stance that appeals to poor, alienated whites, especially males, who feel they have been forgotten. White militant racists talk freely of conflict, even of race war.

Source: Michael Riley Janesville, "White and Wrong," *Time* magazine 140, no.1 (July 6, 1992): 26–27.

18. Even In Rhode Island

The growth and legitimization of the Klan in the early 1920s was felt everywhere in the country, even in the Northeast, where people were and continue to be considered among the most tolerant and liberal-minded in the United States.

No longer was Klan activity limited to the backwoods of the rural South. It had spread into the cities and small towns of Northern America. The huge majority was taken in by the family values and civic responsibility not prone to violence espoused by the new Klan. And when the violence of the Klan, including the attack of Madge Oberholtzer by Indiana Grand Wizard David Curtis Stephenson, was exposed in the media in the mid-1920s, nearly all those moderate members became disgusted and disenchanted and left the organization in droves.

Until then, however, Klan activity sprouted up everywhere, including the small town of Smithfield, Rhode Island. In 1999, local dentist Dr. Daniel Russell was asked to present his recollections of the curious sight of white-robed friends and neighbors gathering in the countryside. He was a mere child at the time, but he still recalled watching the ghost-like Klan figures from afar.

Growing up in the Smithfield countryside, Dr. Daniel Russell glimpsed one of the seldom-told chapters in local history.

On summer Saturday nights, he and a friend would scramble up to the roof of the icehouse in the back yard and peer across Georgiaville Pond.

They climbed at dusk, because that's when the people in the field on the other side—the adults in ghostly white—lit the fiery cross.

"It was certainly something to see," recalls Russell, 79, a retired dentist. "We couldn't hear what they were saying, but they'd have a big meeting and then they'd burn a cross. They had on these white robes and they would parade around. We used to kind of laugh."

As the flames died, the two boys would climb down and run home, as if sensing they had witnessed something they were not meant to see. They probably need not have worried about their safety. Those hooded marchers were almost certainly neighbors.

In 1920s Rhode Island, especially in the rural towns of the Northwest, a new force captured the allegiance of townspeople. The

Knights of the Ku Klux Klan spread their anti-Catholic, anti-immigrant, and anti-black venom among a welcoming populace.

Klan gatherings were as common as clambakes and often drew a comparable crowd.

Beginning in 1925, when an estimated 2,000 people assembled for the state's first Klan wedding, the Klan Field in Georgiaville drew regular gatherings. . . . Their white hoods masked bankers, merchants and even town officials.

Not all Rhode Islanders embraced the Klan. In fact, evidence suggests most rejected the secret order and expressed disgust with its ideals. But the so-called Invisible Empire was popular enough in June 1924 to draw 8,000 people to a monster rally behind Foster Town Hall.

Source: Robert L. Smith, "In the 1920s, the Klan Ruled the Countryside," *The Rhode Island Century,* April 26, 1999. http://www.projo.com/specials/century/month4/426nw1.htm (accessed February 13, 2009).

19. Outgrowing The Klan

One of the most fascinating stories of a Klansman who renounced the organization and shed himself of the hatred and vigilance that gripped him for many years was that of former Indiana Grand Dragon Brad Thompson. Thompson quit the Klan in the late 1990s and even co-authored an exposé on the KKK, Under the Hood: Unmasking the Modern Ku Klux Klan. *In that book, he describes his transformation from rabid Klansman to anti-Klansman.*

Thompson became disenchanted with his fellow Indiana Klansmen, whom he claimed were heavily into drugs and guns. He also feared for his safety at Klan rallies, including one in Pittsburgh on April 5, 1997. Thompson spoke of that rally at the moment in which he finally shed his loyalty to the Klan in his heart and in his mind. He saw 12,000 anti-Klan protesters in front of him. Half of them were angry blacks and all of them were screaming and cursing at him and his fellow Klansmen. That day, he read in a newspaper article that a Pittsburgh Catholic church had held a special mass to pray for the Klansmen. Thompson had been trying to reconnect with his spiritual roots and the fact that members of a Catholic church had prayed for those in a traditionally anti-Catholic organization

tugged at his heartstrings. He considered the hatred he confronted in Pitts-
burgh as a sign from God and finally decided to get out of the Klan, as his
words from the following excerpt from Under the Hood: Unmasking the
Modern Ku Klux Klan *explains.*

I had spent nearly three years giving freely of hate to thousands
and thousands of people. Thousands of people that I didn't even
know. Now I heard God telling me it was my turn.

I don't think anyone is really Klan material when you think about
it, because the Klan just isn't what it says it is. It's all about petty jeal-
ousies and greed. It's all about feeling important at someone else's
expense.

. . . I'd laid in bed, night after night, wide awake consumed in
grief, trying to figure out what possessed me to allow the Klan to capture the heart of my very soul. I still don't know how to answer that.

. . . I still don't understand why I supported an organization, with
all of my effort for almost three years, that has committed so many
crimes against humanity. I'll never be able to explain that. I know I'm
nearly wore out trying.

What I hope, no, what I pray for, is that my experiences, telling
about them, will save some poor soul from the trouble of going
through the same things I've went through.

Believe me, when you pour out hate, you get it back ten fold. And
if you're anywhere near a normal person, then you are left feeling nothing but empty and drained. It's not a good feeling. It's not worth it.

Being in the Klan is like watching a fire in an old dry field. You
burn fast, tall and hot. And when the fire passes, nothing is left inside
you but gray, dusty ashes.

Source: Worth H. Weller with Brad Thompson, *Under the Hood: Unmasking*
the Modern Ku Klux Klan (North Manchester, Ind.: DeWitt Books, 1998), 92–
93, 96.

20. Not Ready For The Grave?

History tells us that one must be wary of a potentially premature burial of
the Ku Klux Klan. The KKK was disbanded in the 1870s, only to be res-
urrected in 1915. It was left for dead in the 1930s, but revitalized during
the civil rights movement. It was considered a thing of the past in the early

1970s and revived again by David Duke and issues such as busing and affirmative action.

But by the 1990s, those who claimed the Klan would never rise again appeared to have greater justification than those who had previously done so. White exposure to blacks in all aspects of society had increased the tolerance of whites to blacks and vice versa. The civil rights laws of the 1960s had taken hold, allowing blacks to begin assuming their rightful place in American society. It resulted in a growing black middle class and huge influx of blacks into white-collar professions, which shrunk black ghettos and rates of violent crime. That, in turn, gave the Klan and other hate groups far less ammunition in their battle to try to prove that a race war was necessary and imminent.

In addition, by the 1990s the Klan was thought of as downright old-fashioned even by the most racist Americans. More sophisticated and militant organizations such as the Aryan Nations had captured the imagination of the younger and most-violently bigoted activists. Klan membership had shrunk so greatly that it had all but disappeared in the South. Just a sprinkling of Klansmen remained and many of them resided in blue-collar Midwestern towns.

The possibility that we have seen the permanent downfall of the Klan was raised in the following article published by the Christian Science Monitor.

Though the KKK has faded as a force, other white supremacy groups that many experts consider even more insidious have risen in the South.

"The problem with the Klan is that it has 136 years of bad history to contend with," says Mark Pitcavage of the Anti-Defamation League. "There's a lot of stigma attached to it, and the rituals and the clothing seem . . . a little more goofy" to today's hate-group adherents.

But it's hard to overlook the import of America's first hate group. From its frivolous beginnings in 1865, the Klan has waxed and waned several times, and its history is marked by periods of terror and violence.

From 5 million members in its heyday in the 1920s, the Klan has declined steadily since the mid-80s to today's 6,000 members.

"The sad truth—well, not so sad—is that the Klan today is almost universally despised," says Mark Potok, editor of the *Intelligence Report* of the Southern Poverty Law Center in Montgomery, Ala., which tracks hate groups. "Even the radical right sees them as . . . a sorry bunch of fools sitting in cow pastures with dunce caps on their heads."

Source: Kris Axtman, "How the South Outgrew the Klan," *Christian Science Monitor* 93, no. 112 (May 4, 2001): 1. http://www.rickross.com/reference/kkk/kkk32.html.

Selected Bibliography

Books

Blee, Kathleen M. *Women of the Klan*. Los Angeles: University of California Press, 1991.

Ezekiel, Raphael S. *The Racist Mind*. New York: Penguin Books, 1995.

Kennedy, Stetson. *I Rode with the Ku Klux Klan*. London: Arco Publishing, 1954.

Klein, Shelley. *The Most Evil Secret Societies in History*. London: Michael O'Mara Books, 2005.

MacLean, Nancy. *Behind the Mask of Chivalry: The Making of the Second Ku Klux Klan*. New York: Oxford University Press, 1994.

Ridgeway, James. *Blood in the Face: The Ku Klux Klan, Aryan Nations, Nazi Skinheads, and the Rise of the New White Culture*. New York: Basic Books, 1996.

Sims, Patsy. *The Klan*. Lexington, Ky.: The University Press of Kentucky, 1996.

Tucker, Richard K. *The Dragon and the Cross*. Hamden, Conn.: The Shoe String Press, 1991.

Wade, Wyn Craig. *The Fiery Cross: The Ku Klux Klan in America*, New York: Simon and Schuster, 1987.

Internet Sites

Anti-Defamation League Online, "About the Ku Klux Klan: Extremism in America," http://www.adl.org/learn/ext_us/kkk/default.asp?LEARN_Cat=Extremism& LEARN_SubCat=Extremism_in_America&xpicked=4&item=kkk.

Federal Bureau of Investigation, "Ku Klux Klan," http://foia.fbi.gov/foiaindex/kkk.htm.

Ku Klux Klan homepage, "The Ku Klux Klan," http://www.kukluxklan.bz/.

PBS Online, "The Rise and Fall of Jim Crow," http://www.pbs.org/wnet/jim crow/stories_org_kkk.html.

Video

The Ku Klux Klan: A Secret History (The History Channel), 1998. (Released on DVD in 2005).

Mississippi Burning, MGM (1988).

Ghosts of Mississippi, Turner Home Entertainment (1996).

Index

About the Author

MARTIN GITLIN is a freelance book writer and journalist based in Cleveland, Ohio. In addition to *Diana, Princess of Wales: A Biography* (Greenwood 2008) and *Audrey Hepburn: A Biography* (Greenwood 2008), he has written several history books for students, including works on the landmark Brown v. Board of Education case, Battle of Little Bighorn and the Stock Market Crash of 1929. He has also written biographies of NASCAR drivers Jimmie Johnson and Jeff Gordon. Gitlin worked for two decades as a sportswriter, during which time he won more than 45 awards, including first place for general excellence from Associated Press. That organization also selected him as one of the top four feature writers in Ohio.